D1143042

The Development of
British Transport Networks

BRIAN FULLERTON

Theory and Practice in Geography

OXFORD UNIVERSITY PRESS · 1975

Oxford University Press, Ely House, London W. 1

GLASGOW NEW YORK TORONTO MELBOURNE WELLINGTON
CAPE TOWN IBADAN NAIROBI DAR ES SALAAM LUSAKA ADDIS ABABA
DELHI BOMBAY CALCUTTA MADRAS KARACHI LAHORE DACCA
KUALA LUMPUR SINGAPORE HONG KONG TOKYO

ISBN 0 19 874032 8

© Oxford University Press 1975

Printed in Great Britain
by J. W. Arrowsmith Ltd., Bristol

Contents

List of figures

1 Introduction

The development of the British transport system during the last two centuries has an intrinsic interest for professional students and for amateurs. The ingenuity which carried canals across physical barriers and the enterprise with which the railway network was built contributed to Britain's brief period of leadership in the technical development of 'western' civilization. Monuments of the heroic period of transport development surround us. Millions travel to work every day on pioneer railway lines. Many of the original bridges, tunnels, and flights of locks are still in use. Few people live more than 80 km from a famous transport artefact or the site of a major innovation in transport technique. Museums and preservation societies maintain and rebuild steamships, steam engines, and working railway lines in all parts of the country in order that something of the vigour of the past may be recaptured by the present generation. In the simplified form in which the story is often told, the activity of a small group of men, remarkable for their single-minded purpose and energy, stands in marked contrast to conditions in our own time when the further development of British transport is apparently restrained by the inertia of committees of inquiry, the parsimony of the Treasury, and the inconsistencies of decisions made by successive governments.

Transport history involves much more than organized nostalgia, for studies in the growth and expansion of particular transport systems may lead to the formulation of general models of development, which, in further comparison with the historical course of events, draw attention to significant characteristics of individual networks. Such work has clear relevance to present-day planning for our future needs in such controversial issues as the extension of the motorway network and the location of any new airports.

Interest in the story of the actual development of transport in Britain is stimulated by an extensive and rapidly expanding literature which includes excellent modern biographies and economic, social, technical, and institutional histories. Geographical studies, although relatively few in number, throw a distinctive light on the scene, complementing the work of some social and economic historians in discussing long-term problems which still have relevance today. These include the interaction between transport and other sectors of the economy with the associated competition for capital, and the interplay of conflicting interest groups, and also the effects of a drastic reduction of travel time and cost on the spread of ideas and the development of institutions.

This book is designed as a short geographical introduction to the development of transport in Britain, which introduces some of the relevant theoretical approaches and also indicates material found in historical, economic, and technical studies which geographers may find interesting. It is a study of historical networks and of their influences in shaping the transport systems of today. For a comprehensive under-standing of the topics which are discussed students should first consult the further reading suggested at the end of this book and then move on to the extensive literature in journals listed in the references. Certain transport media, including pipelines and cable transport in the twentieth century, and areas of study including urban transport in the nineteenth century, are omitted here but may be studied through the recommended literature.

This introductory survey deals in broad historical and geographical categories. Time is measured in decades although many significant changes took place within them. It is only with the benefit of hind-sight that the 1830s and 1920s are seen to have experienced major shifts in transport development. The terms *local, intercity* and *international* are used to represent three orders of distance and interaction. Local trips are those which take place within a conurbation or within the hinterland of a rural service centre, extending at most to distances of 50 km. Intercity journeys occur between one large town and another, which in Britain involves distances of between 100 and 800 km. International movements have their origin or destination abroad via sea or airport. The majority of journeys fit these categories; the others require more elaborate descrip-tion than there is space for here.

A similar simple distinction is made between *line-haul* and *feeder/distributor* routes. Many goods and passenger movements may be formalized as three-stage journeys involving (1) the movement of units of an assembly point relatively near to their points of origin; (2) the bulking of units and their transfer to a distribution point which is relatively near to their destinations; (3) the disaggregation of the units and the final distribution to their destinations. There may be a break of bulk and/or a *modal split* (a transfer from one mode of transport to another) at the assembly and distribution point. The second (line-haul) stage of the journey is normally longer than the other stages and involves a larger vehicle.

The study of transport systems has given rise to some specialized vocabulary. Transport engineers, planners, and operators are not yet fully agreed on which of the alternative technical terms to employ for certain elements but those listed here are in widespread current use. Alternative expressions are given in brackets. A transport *system* may be defined as the sum of transport facilities and modes available within an area, including all terminal facilities, offices, and fuel supply points. Types of transport, e.g. road, rail, inland water, sea, and air, are described as *modes*. In areas where there is considerable linkage between the transport modes the transport system may be said to be *integrated*. Individual transport links are called *routes* (edges, vectors). The intersecting routes of a transport mode form a *network* and the junction of routes of one or modes is termed a *node* (vertex). For comparative purposes it is sometimes advisable to transform networks into formalized graphs so that their properties may be isolated and assessed separately. Any disconnected routes in the system are known as *subgraphs*. Graphs disregard the length and sinuosities of routes in their emphasis on shape.

Geographers have studied transport routes and buildings as features in the contemporary cultural landscape of Britain (Appleton 1962) and have sought explanations for present-day patterns of routes in studies of the contemporary geography of the late eighteenth and early nineteenth centuries (Smith 1949). They have recently extended their attention beyond the actual areal differentiation of the earth towards systematic investigation of the basic spatial attributes of phenomena. There has been a renewal of interest in the geometrical description of transport networks and in the efficiency of such networks to satisfy quantifiable criteria such as the maximum linkage of places or maximum throughput of vehicles.

The spatial study of a transport system is concerned with both the potential of the system and with actual patterns of movement along the routes. The potential value of a transport system may be expressed in terms of the *accessibility* which it offers within its area of operation. Development and extension of a transport system are invariably undertaken in order to improve accessibility in one way or another. Accessibility may be calculated from one point in the system (*particular* accessibility) or from a large number of points (*general* accessibility). It may be measured in units of space, time, or cost. In the analysis of accessibility three factors, shape, density, capacity, are of paramount importance. *Shape* relates to the pattern of routes and nodes; *density* to the proximity of routes and nodes to each other. Shape and density together determine the spatial efficiency of a network—how well it fills the space it was constructed to serve. It is important to distinguish between those transport networks which were built to satisfy indentified and measured demand for links between specific places and innovating networks whose development and extension were essentially speculative.

Since maximum linkage and maximum throughput are unlikely to be achieved over the whole of a transport system, it is useful to know the original purpose of the system and the resources available to the builders. The *capacity* of a route or network, a function of its technology, measures how much traffic it can carry at any one time.

Traffic flows, the actual patterns of movement along the routes, reveal the extent to which the potential accessibility of a transport system is realized and show how the transport system contributes to the spatial efficiency of the economy which it serves. Attempts to push too much traffic through the system lead to congestion and delay. Under-utilization of a transport system may occur for a variety of reasons. There may be too many routes for the available traffic or too many modes may be competing for it. The volume of traffic rises and falls with the general prosperity of the economy. Many transport routes are built in expectation of demand and it may be some time before traffic rises to match the installed capacity of the system. The world is full of transport investments which never realized the hopes of their promoters. The financial solvency or profits of transport modes and systems are important general measures of their efficiency in relation to other parts of the economy, but so is the service rendered by transport to the community. Geographers have a more limited concern with the spatial efficiency of transport and the selection of criteria to measure it.

The interest in the analysis of spatial patterns which forms such a marked feature of modern geography has extended but not replaced a long-established interest in aspects of areal differentiation—in this case the effects of the shape of the land and the pattern of distribution of its resources on the more mobile elements of the economy. New transport developments are partially constrained by the existing transport provision, but the shape of Britain and the layout of its major uplands have favoured the repeated choice of certain routes and discouraged the development of others.

Route systems could be designed for Britain on two principles: *administrative* to link London with the chief regional centres of the country and to provide routes to the ports which link Britain with her neighbours, or *economic* to serve the maximum population with the maximum of route kilometres. The primary routes on Fig. 1 link London (which has been the predominant city since Roman times) with the western English conurbations (A, E), Scotland (A, B, F), Wales (D), Ireland (A, C), France via the Channel Ports (G) or Solent (H), and the Netherlands (I). These routes total 1550 km. A further 1250 km of secondary routes extend this network to the remaining regions. These comprise a northern extension of Route E from the West Midlands and

Lancashire to Clydeside, routes from the West Midlands to South West England (J) and South Wales (K), also east-west links from the West Midlands to the East Midlands and East Anglia (L), from Lancashire to Yorkshire (M), Cumbria to North East England (N) and Clydeside to Aberdeen (O). A minimum route system linking the regions of Britain and the short-sea ports would have a length of 2800 km.

The effect of population distribution on route length is shown by the graph inserted in Fig. 1. Route length is plotted against the proportion of the population it might serve if designed for that purpose alone. The curve was calculated in relation to the distribution of population in 1971 and shows the percentage of population which could be reached by progressively extending a transport network from London to other parts of Britain. Population 'served' by the network is defined as that living within 9 km of a route. If the route were a railway or motorway, with limited access points along it, the effective distance of the route from many of the population would be greater than 9 km. Thus almost 11 million people, 20 per cent of the population of Britain, live within 9 km of a direct route from London to Birmingham of 180 km. Further extension of the network would 'reach' smaller but still substantial proportions of the population and 80 per cent of the population would be 'reached' before extension of the network gave a less than proportionate increase in the population served. The shape of Britain and the distribution pattern of its population are such that the 'primary' route network of 1550 km suggested on Fig. 1 would reach to within 9 km of half the population and the total network of 2800 km to within 70 per cent. To serve the most remote 20 per cent of the population an additional network of over 6000 km would be required.

Although the distribution of population in 1971 was more highly concentrated than it had ever been before and more route kilometres would have been needed to reach a given proportion of the population in 1800, the basic principle described by the curve is of fairly general application. At most times and in most countries a relatively large proportion of the population can be reached by a simple system of routes between the largest regional cities. A route system built to serve either the administrative or the economic principle goes a long way towards serving the other. If, however, a transport system is required to reach every village, the total network will be very much longer than the interregional network.

Fig. 1 therefore sketches the fundamental constraints on transport provision suggested by the shape of Britain and the distribution of its major resources and population. The following chapters describe the

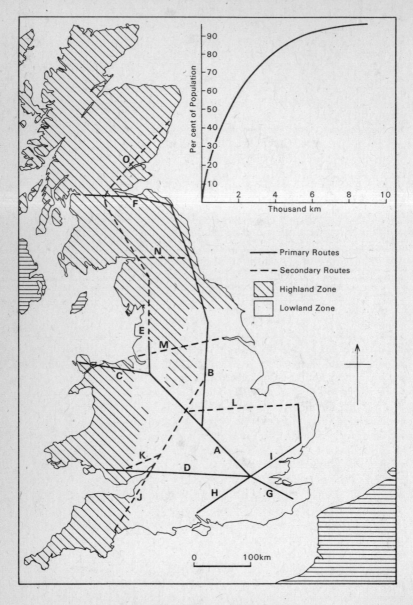

Fig. 1. British transport—basic geography

actual development of transport networks during the last two centuries and show how deeply the underlying rationale of British geography was often buried under other considerations.

2 Inland waterways 1750-1830

The first nationally organized transport system in Britain was developed by the Romans between 100 and 400 A.D. The Roman roads, of which 8000 km have been discovered, were 'obviously planned to serve the needs of conquest and government rather than those of civil traffic. The whole system radiates from London, and gives the impression of having been designed so as to provide the most direct communication from point to point of a network whose nodal points are the *coloniae,* the legionary fortresses, and the tribal capitals' (Collingwood and Myres 1936, p. 240). This system was of limited use for other traffic and so fell into disuse during the fourteen centuries before 1800 when most people's needs were satisfied within their immediate neighbourhood and the few long-distance journeys on land were made along end-on combinations of local routeways.

Although there was no co-ordinated route system equivalent to the *routes nationales* of France (a network of 27 000 km) in the eighteenth century, trunk routes of very variable surface and capacity, as described in John Ogilby's *Britannia* (1675) extended over 11 400 km in England and Wales, giving 1 km of highway per 11 km^2 in the Lowland zone and 1 km per 17 km^2 in the Highland zone.

The importance of rivers for communication is shown by the way in which the majority of counties in the English lowlands, most of which were established in the tenth century, comprise parts of river basins. By the early eighteenth century, as Fig. 2 shows, after deepening and rectification work ('navigations') on the middle reaches of many rivers, their potential transport capacity had been almost fully realized. The benefits of river transport were virtually confined to the basins of the Thames, Fen rivers, Humber, and Severn in the English Midlands although many estuaries penetrated a few kilometres inland from the southern, north-eastern and western coasts. The bulk of Highland Britain and significant plateau regions of the Lowland zone could only be reached by carts or pack-horses.

Much of the new manufacturing industry of the eighteenth century was in fact located on the plateaux which form the transition between the Lowland and Highland zones in Britain. Here coal began to replace charcoal in iron smelting and water power was harnessed to increase the output of textiles (originally organized as a scattered domestic industry relying on pack-horse transport).

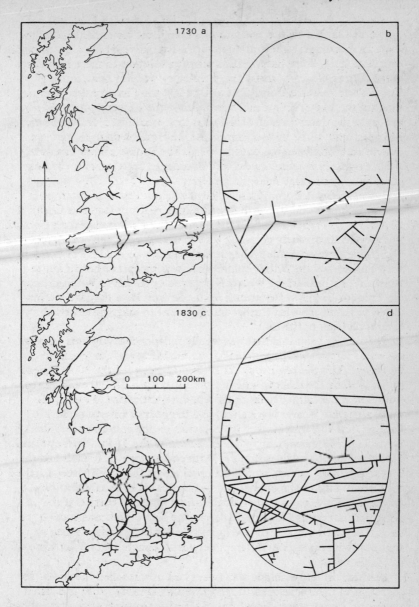

Fig. 2. Inland waterways 1730 and 1830

The cargo of a 30-ton river barge could fill 50 carts or load 100 pack-horses, so that the cost of transport for even short distances beyond the shore or river banks almost prohibited the assembly of bulky raw materials on a large scale. Some industrialists sought a solution to these high costs in the cutting of short canals. The technology was not new for the Romans had built the Fossdyke Canal to link the Trent to the Wash via Lincoln, the Exeter Ship Canal was begun in the sixteenth century, while in France the Canal du Midi (1681) was long established. European canals had been built in the hope of improving the trade of their district and *general* accessibility to the outside world. The British narrow canals of the late eighteenth century were built in order to carry specific cargoes cheaply, to particular mines and factories.

Josiah Wedgwood, for instance, ownded a pottery near outcrops of coal and ganister clay in North Staffordshire 70 km inland at a height of 122 m. He also needed flints from Gravesend and china clay from Cornwall transported successively in sailing vessels, river barges, and road wagons. The fragile finished products began their journey to markets in London, West Europe and the British colonies overseas by cart either 32 km to Winsford, the head of the Weaver Navigation or 42 km to Willingdon on the Trent or 68 km to Bridgnorth on the Severn. Here they were transferred to river barges for further transhipment to seagoing vessels at Liverpool, Hull, or Bristol.

The first British canal that was wholly independent of rivers (except for water supply) was dug in 1757 from the Mersey 15 km north to St. Helens. This Sankey Brook canal (Fig. 3) ascended the 30 m plateau by locks along the shallow valley of the Sankey Brook and enabled coal from South Lancashire to reach the Cheshire saltfields (24 km to the south along the Weaver Navigation) and the port of Liverpool. In 1761 the Earl of Bridgewater linked his collieries on the eastern edge of the South Lancashire coalfield with Manchester by the 16 km Worsley Canal. This canal, built by James Brindley, with embankments, tunnels and the Barton aqueduct (which carried the canal across the Irwell Valley), halved the price of coal in Manchester and demonstrated in Britain that canals, though expensive to construct, could breach physical barriers if the potential traffic was adequate to defray the high initial construction costs. They were capable of development as an independent mode of transport with essentially different network characteristics from those of navigable rivers.

In historical terms, inland waterways had now reached the end of the first stage in their development recognized by Girard (1965) and called *symbiosis.* In this stage a new form of transport extends (river navigations)

LOCATION

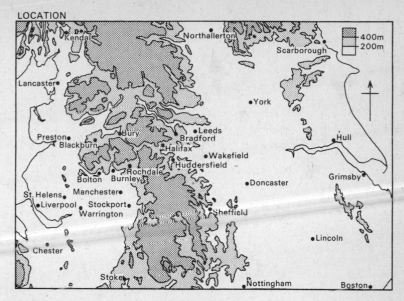

INLAND WATERWAYS 1830

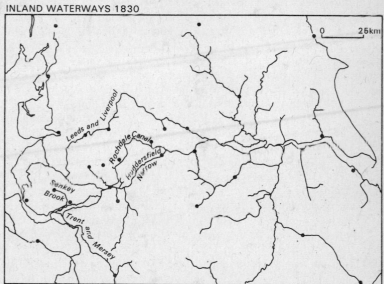

Fig. 3. Northern England: inland waterways 1830

and complements (canals) an existing transport mode (natural waterways) with break of bulk at the nodes where the new system joins the old.

The Bridgewater canal (1767, from Manchester to Runcorn) was followed by the Trent and Mersey Canal (Fig. 3b; 1766—77) across the main English waterparting. This canal of 150 km joined the Weaver Navigation to the Trent, crossing a spur of the Pennines at Harecastle at a summit elevation of 120 m by a tunnel of 2·1 km. Further to the north, the Rochdale Canal (1794—1804) linked the Bridgewater canal with the Humber drainage basin. The Leeds and Liverpool canal (1777—1816) sought a low watershead by a rather circuitous northern route of 259 km and 104 locks. The Huddersfield Narrow Canal (1794—1811) had a more direct route of 193 km between Leeds and Liverpool but climbed to 195 m with 147 locks and a tunnel of 5 km under the Standedge plateau.

On the West Midland plateau a system of contour canals at different elevations was built. They were linked to each other by locks, and further long flights of locks, as at Tardebigge, connected the system to the Trent and Severn.

These early canals had limited and essentially industrial objectives. Of the 165 Canal Acts passed between 1758 and 1803, 137 served mines and ironworks. The success of the canals in the North and Midlands of England, where they played an essential role in the process of industrialization, led to their extension to other parts of Britain where their immediate relevance was less apparent. London, with its one million population, was handling three-quarters of the foreign trade of Britain and formed the focus of the canals of southern England. The Thames and Severn Canal (1789) was followed by the London and Birmingham Canal (1790), the Grand Junction Canal (1805), and the Wey and Arun (1816) to Chichester, to provide new water comunications in each major direction.

In Scotland the Forth and Clyde Canal (1768—90) from Clydeside to Grangemouth was extended to Edinburgh by the Forth Union Canal (1821). The Government built the Crinan (1801) and Caledonian (1822) Canals as measures of regional development in the Scottish Highlands. It was hoped that the improved accessibility of the Great Glen would encourage private investment there and that the avoidance of the long and dangerous sea routes round the Mull of Kintyre and Cape Wrath would increase the prosperity of fishing and the coasting trade.

In terms of the historical cycles of development proposed by Girard the period from about 1790 to 1830 is one in which canals predominated goods transport. In its *predominant* stage a transport mode, whatever its initial function, is adopted almost universally to compete with or to replace older modes. There is considerable prospective extension of the network in the hope rather than in the promise of traffic. Few of the canals of southern England ever paid their way. During this period the essentially local capital and enterprise which characterized the early British canals was replaced by a more general investment and shareholding in which the London capital market came to play a dominating part.

By 1830, however, Britain had 6500 km of navigable inland waterways. The over-all density was 1 km to 47 km^2 in Highland Britain and 1 km to 18 km^2 in Lowland Britain. Figure 3c shows that although the canals originated on the fringes of Highland Britain they penetrated no great distance inland except in the southern Pennines, in South Wales, and in the Central Lowlands of Scotland. Some coalfields, notably that of North East England where plateaux reached the coast, derived no benefit from canals. The primary routes suggested in Figure 1 were served by canals except from London to the Channel Ports (G) and the longer-distance routeways through Highland Britain to Ireland (C) and Scotland (B and E).

The actual network of British water transport in the early eighteenth century (Fig. 2a) is stylized into a graph in Fig. 2b. The circumference of the graph represents coastal shipping and the internal straight lines represent rivers and river navigations. On Fig. 2b there are 38 routes and 35 nodes, of which 22 represent coastal ports where goods had to be transshipped from barges to seagoing vessels.

The ease with which one part of a graph may be reached from any other part is described as its *connectivity*. The simplest measure of connectivity is the number of *circuits* (routes from any node to any other node). This is expressed in the *cyclomatic number* and obtained by subtracting from the number of routes (e) the number of nodes (v) and adding the number of graphs or subgraphs (p). By this measure the connectivity of the British water transport system in the mid-eighteenth century is very low:

$$e - v + p = \mu \quad 38 - 35 + 1 = 4.$$

In 1830 (Fig. 2d) there were 161 routes and 121 nodes, giving a cyclomatic number (μ) of 41 (= 161 − 121 + 1) compared with a cyclomatic number of 4 in 1730. The small number of points where canals crossed each other without interchange as at the Barton aqueduct on the Bridgewater canal are not apparent on Fig. 3d. The cyclomatic number measures one aspect of connectivity, other indices analyse the situation a little further. The number of routes between places as a percentage of the maximum possible number of routes is measured by the gamma index (γ). In the simplest network three nodes may be linked by a minimum of two routes, but three routes are required to link each node directly to the other two. The addition of each successive node to this simple network increases the maximum number of routes possible by three. The maximum number of routes in a system may therefore be expressed as $3(v - 2)$ and the gamma index becomes $\frac{e}{3(v-2)}$. In Fig. 2b the gamma index is $\frac{38}{3(35-2)} = 38$ per cent, but by 1830 (Fig. 2d) the gamma index for the British waterway system had risen to 45 per cent. The *alpha index* (α) measures the number of circuits as a percentage of the possible number of circuits. As routes are added to a minimum network, more circuits are made available. The maximum number of routes is $3(v - 2)$ and the minimum number of routes is one less than the number of nodes $(v - 1)$. The maximum number of circuits must therefore be $3(v - 2) - (v - 1) = 2v - 5$. As the actual number of circuits (the cyclomatic number) is $e - v + 1$ the alpha index is $\frac{e - v + 1}{2v - 5}$. In 1730 the alpha index for the British waterway system was $\frac{38 - 35 + 1}{2(35 - 5)} = \frac{4}{60} = 7$ per cent. By 1830 the alpha index had risen to 18 per cent, still a rather loosely integrated network.

Fig. 3 brings the network of inland waterways in 1830 into closer focus by concentrating on a representative cross-section of Britain between the Irish Sea and the Humber, including upland and lowland, early industrial, coalfield, late industrial, and rural landscapes. The canal network in this area illustrates the alternative solutions to basic route M linking the Mersey and the Humber, the extent to which navigations extended the useful waterways upstream into the Yorkshire and Derbyshire coalfield, and the use of the northern tributaries of the Humber in the service of an agricultural economy. As the area covered by Fig. 3 includes parts of the Highland and Lowland zones of Britain the density of inland waterways, 27 km^2 per kilometre of waterway, is intermediate. The cyclomatic number of the routes shown in Fig. 3 is 10, much lower than that of the British waterway system as a whole. The alpha index at 37 per cent is much higher but the gamma index is lower. As the predominant traffic moved between individual mines or ports and factories sited along the waterways so the pattern of the network consists, in graph language, of *paths* (routes between A and B only) and *trees* (routes between A and B, A and C, A and D, and so forth) with relatively few *circuits* (routes allowing general circulation between A, B, C, and D).

As in Britain as a whole, the canals in the North of England improved particular accessibility in terms of time and of journeys and the cost per ton carried. Their contribution to the improvement of general accessibility was restricted by their sparse distribution which necessitated many road feeder routes and time-consuming load and unloading of the barges. A further problem was posed by the presence of three types of vessel.

Coastal sailing boats, barges, and narrow boats were each restricted to their own waterways. On the inland waterways, barge canals, generally 5 m wide, predominanted in southern England and provided the two northern Pennine crossings. The canals of the West Midlands and Cheshire, which provided most of the connecting links between regions, were 2·4 m wide and could only take narrow boats. On barge and narrow canals, with the exception of the Leeds and Liverpool, locks were 18–21 m long. The rate structure for long-distance carriage of goods was even more fragmented and there were, for instance, no through canal rates between London and Birmingham until 1897. These factors, together with the low speeds attained (3–5 km per hour depending on type of cargo and the number of locks on the route) seriously limited the capacity of the canal network for long-distance transport.

The effect of canal transport on the relocation of industry and population was limited by the short period of forty years during which it predominated in the transport system. Canals halved the cost of carriage along their routes, facilitating the use of coal rather than water-wheels to drive the machinery which was being invented during the latter half of the eighteenth century. Although factories were still few, the opportunities for relatively cheap fuel fostered their linear concentration along canal banks. Some of these factories are still to be found in the valleys of Lancashire, West Yorkshire, and South Wales, between Wolverhampton and Birmingham and along the Regent's Canal and the Lea in north London. By about 1830 railways began to challenge the predominant position of canals in the transport system. Canals soon passed into the third or *auxiliary,* as Girard (1965) terms it, historical stage of their development. Inland waterways became subsidiary to the railway and only effectively used by a limited number of commodities travelling over a part of their network.

3 Railway development 1830-50

One of the most interesting questions is why the railway came to dominate transport between 1830 and the First World War. The individual elements of the railway were being tested and assembled during the 1820s with increasing success at the same time as experiements with vehicles to run on existing roads met with discouragement and failure. Once the railway demonstrated its ability to carry large numbers of goods and passengers rapidly, it came to monopolize transport investment and invention for fifty years.

In the history and geography of the British railway network the stage of *symbiosis,* characterized by railways as feeders to other modes of transport and a pattern of short, isolated routes, lasted until about 1830.

Plateways of various kinds had existed for centuries on the European coalfields in order to ease the haulage of the laden coal wagons by horses. Some of these plateways, most notably in North East England, where coal was mined up to 300 m altitude and 13 km distance from tidewater, used gravity-worked inclines and stationary haulage engines. The railway made its debut as a new transport mode when plates were replaced by rails, stationary by locomotive engines, and when general cargo and passengers were carried as well as coal. All these features characterized the Stockton and Darlington Railway of 1825 although its essential purpose was to link a group of coal-pits with the river port of Stockton. Many similar routes were built, still primarily concerned with bringing coal to an inland market (Leicester and Swannington 1832), canal bank (Monkland and Kirkintilloch 1826), or seaport. The Liverpool and Manchester railway, which heralded the dominance of railways over all other modes of land transport, was first mooted in 1797, surveyed in 1824, and completed in 1830. It was the first railway to rely completely on steam power and to perform all the services of a common carrier. The route from Liverpool to Manchester was now served by trains running at 32 km per hour rather than canal barges at 3–5 k.p.h. The cost of carriage was halved. Passengers soon supplied half the revenue. The railway owned its own track and vehicles. It supplied a comprehensive transport service for a fee rather than providing a means of transport upon which customers moved their own vehicles on payment of toll as on contemporary canals and turnpiked roads.

After the opening of the Stockton and Darlington line in 1825 and the Liverpool and Manchester in 1830 railway construction went ahead very rapidly in Britain (Fig. 4). By about 1835 the younger railway engineers had freed themselves from the traditions of the canals and had adapted their gradients to the rapidly increasing power of the new steam locomotives. Railways freed British transport from the constraints of physical geography, and the speed and enterprise with which this new transport mode was developed were very striking. Between 1830 and 1845 3600 km of route were completed compared with 1600 km during the first fifteen years of the motorway programme in the twentieth century.

During the period from 1830 to 1850 the building of an interregional network of railways signalled railway dominance of the transport system. The first interregional link served Route A on Fig. 1 between Lancashire, the West Midlands, and London. This route was completed in 1838 and within ten years all major British cities were 'on the railway', The completion of the primary and secondary routes involved the construction of tunnels and bridges of then unprecedented size, the first large works of engineering construction since the Roman aqueducts of the first centuries A.D., but railway connection was completed with Edinburgh and Holyhead (for Dublin) in 1850 and with Cardiff in 1852.

The growth of the railway network is shown in Fig. 4. The rapid increase in railway lines during the early 1840s represents the completion of projects started in the early 1830s and before. Fig. 1 shows that the 3600 km of railway mania of 1845–6 could have provided an adequate intercity network and come to within a two-hour horse and cart journey of half the population. In fact, when 10 000 km of railway had been built in 1851 only a triangle east of London, Liverpool, and Newcastle had an adequate network of railways and only tentacles of rail penetrated Scotland, Wales, and southern and south-western England.

The construction of the railways was organized and financed by numerous small groups and each route was subjected to individual Parliamentary scrutiny without reference to any agreed standard of national or regional need. Investment was also irregular. A peak of investment in 1836 during which 1600 km were authorized was followed by a shortage of capital, and then there was a larger frenzy of investment, the 'railway mania' in 1845–6 during with 14 000 km were approved.

The capital cost of construction of the lines was estimated by Clapham (1921) to average £6800 per km in Germany, £10 200 in Belgium, but £21 700 in Britain. In Britain at that time capital was accumulating rapidly and interest rates were relatively low. Railway routes were heavily capitalized and the high costs to the builders, in so far as these related to the bridges, embankments, and tunnels which characterized the British network, were associated with relatively low costs to subsequent users.

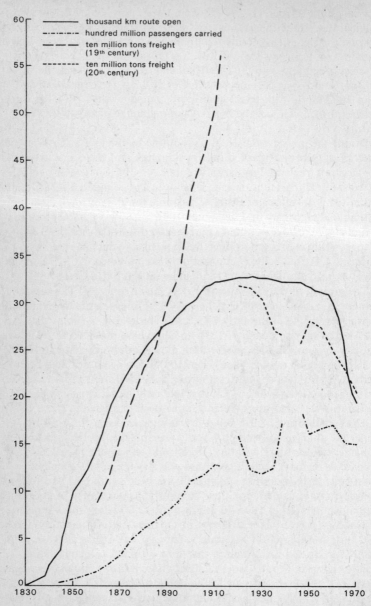

Fig. 4. Railway network length and traffic 1830–1970. Based on Mitchell and Deane (1962).

In most of the rest of the world high interest rates and/or the uncertain prospects of traffic determined that the first railways should be lightly built with steep gradients and tight curves in hill country saving initial cost to the builders at the expense of subsequent costs to users.

Capital was raised by large numbers of relatively small companies subject to the minimum of government legislation during the vital early years. In the atmosphere of excitement, especially during the railway mania of 1845–6, many projects were advanced which had little economic justification in themselves and no relevance to developments proposed elsewhere. Although most of these projects came to grief, the search for quick, small-scale profits prevented the development of any national policy on the layout of the railway network.

The government attempted to bring some order into the spread of the network by establishing a Railway Board in 1844 but the tide of Parliamentary opinion (fortified by a growing railway interest in both Houses) caused the Board to be abandoned in 1845, leaving the government enforcing only maximum charges and minimum standards of safety and service.

A historical explanation of the British railway network must be sought by detailed analyses of the perceptions and activities and numerous groups of promoters operating in the City, at ports, on coalfields, and in rural market towns. In some cases, for instance London–Southampton (Route H on Fig. 1) and Bristol–London (Route D), interregional routes were planned. In other areas, notably along Route B, they emerged as end-on combinations of small coalfield lines.

The influence of individual entrepreneurs on the development of the British railway network was as profound as in any other major innovations. Many of the early engineering consultants attained great prestige and were able to apply their strongly held individual views to the alignment of their routes. The pioneer work of George Stephenson in the development of locomotives led to his appointment as consultant engineer to the Liverpool and Manchester Railway, and his success in crossing the difficult terrain of Chat Moss led to many similar consultancies for himself and his son Robert. The Stephensons had grown up with locomotives of very limited power and designed their roadbed accordingly. They were prepared to deviate, cut, embank, and tunnel on a major scale in order to achieve ruling grades of 0·3 per cent (1 to 330) where possible. When steeper gradients were necessary, as at the approaches to many ports including London, Liverpool, and Glasgow, short steep gradients were built, originally worked by stationary engines. The Tring cutting and other works enabling a ruling grade of 0·3 per cent across the grain of the scarplands between Camden Town and Crewe still remind us of their engineering style. Contemporary engineers who were younger, notably Locke, were much more tolerant of medium gradients. The British loading gauge (outer dimensions of goods wagons and passenger coaches), which is smaller than those of Europe and North America, and the track gauge (width between rails), which is now common to western and central Europe and North America, was also bequeathed by George Stephenson who always advised the 1·435 m gauge of the carts of North East England. The personal influence of the Stephensons thus made itself felt on the first railways of many European countries and, by export of their locomotive, of several American states. The 1·435 gauge was not, at first, universal. Brunel, the engineer of the Great Western Railway from Bristol to London, used a 'broad' gauge of 2·123 m. The breaks of gauge where Great Western lines met those of other companies became an expensive impediment to a national railway network. The 1·435 m gauge was decreed by Parliament in 1846 for all new lines outside Great Western territory. The conversion of Great Western track to the 1·435 m gauge was completed in 1892.

Early railway engineers gave little attention to one of the most interesting problems in transport economics, viz. how far through routes might profitably deviate in order to attract way traffic. This was due either to a healthy respect for physical obstacles ('it would be easy to get a train into Northampton but difficult to get it out again') or faulty intelligence ('the traffic of Huddersfield is not worth a horse and cart'), but gave some scope for duplication of routes in the later, expansionist phase of railway growth.

Railways were pioneered in Britain within a different industrial and economic context from that prevailing in Europe. When the railways were built in Britain there was already a nucleus of factory industry on the coalfields, and the relative decline of the older urban industries of the south and rural Midlands of England was well under way. In Europe the railways came in time to bring coal sufficiently cheaply to existing centres of industry and capital to avoid major and rapid changes in the locations of industries. Few other countries allowed as much freedom for the private development of railways. In Belgium, France and Sweden both the primary routes and the subsequent stages of network development were centrally planned and executed by public and private capital in partnership. In the German lands priority was given to the major interregional routes. Many American railroads had considerable initial state subvention. Although British engineers established railway systems in many foreign countries Britain did not provide a model for the subsequent development of railway networks nor were situations overseas reflected here.

The geographical effects of the virtually unregulated spread of railways may be seen in a characteristic stretch of Britain in Fig. 5. In 1841 the railway network was still somewhat similar in shape to that of the canal network in 1830 (Fig. 3) save that the Pennine tunnels were not yet completed and there was no equivalent to the 'navigations' of the Humber and its tributaries. The agricultural rural areas had virtually no railway service as yet and the lowlands still relied on inland waterways. In terms of interregional routes, Route M (Fig. 1) from Liverpool to Hull was virtually complete and the north-south routes B and E in process of achievement. With only 26 routes as opposed to 104 on the inland waterway system, and 25 nodes on the railways as against 95 on the waterways, the railway still had low connectivity. The cyclomatic number stood at 4, the same as at the beginning of the canal era in 1730. The percentage of routes of possible routes (gamma = 38 per cent) and of circuits of possible circuits (alpha = 4 per cent) had already exceeded those on the inland waterway system.

By 1850 the Pennine crossings had been completed and the railway net spread out, albeit sparsely, across the eastern rural areas. All the towns marked on Fig. 3 had railway links, the cyclomatic number had risen to 67, the gamma index to 56 per cent and the alpha index to 35 per cent (Table 1). The network still concentrated on the connection of main towns but there were already alternative lines along Route M between the West Riding towns and Manchester.

Fig. 5 like Fig. 3, exaggerates the connectivity of the system, for just as there were different lock dimensions on the canals so there were many railway companies. Twenty-eight companies operated in the areas shown in Fig. 5 in 1850, some of which formed working entities with their neighbours. All had the same gauge but the through working of wagons between companies was not well developed until the 1870s despite the establishment of the Railway Clearing House in 1845.

The advent of the railways in the 1830s consigned inland waterways to a third phase in their history as *auxiliary* to other modes in the system. Railways proved superior in moving goods from a much wider variety of locations, faster, at more regular speeds, and with a lower outlay of man and horsepower per ton. On many routes the railway companies bought up competing canals in order to close them or to run them for supplementary traffic. Thus the era of canal dominance had lasted for less than a century in Britain. In marked contrast to developments on the European mainland, where the network of high-capacity canals is still slowly expanding, only one canal was cut after the wide Gloucester and Berkeley of 1827. This was the Manchester Ship Canal of 1886–94, built at the height of Lancashire's prosperity.

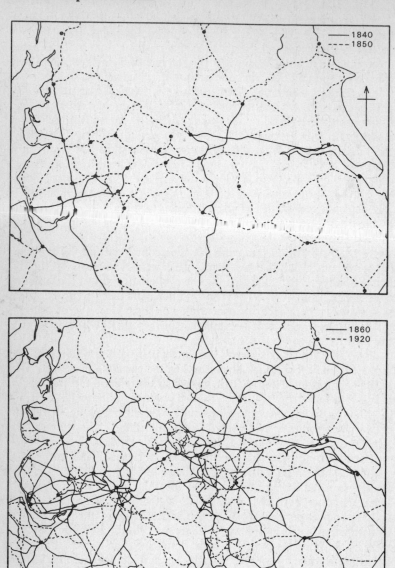

Fig. 5. Northern England: railways 1840–1920. For key to locations see Fig. 3.

The traffic carried on the canals showed no substantial change when the network ceased to expand further; and from the 1880s until the First World War maintained a level of 35 million tons per annum. The average distance travelled per ton of cargo remained at 28 km, illustrating the limited role of canals as short-distance movers of bulk commodities between ports, factories, and warehouses established upon their banks.

4 The railway age 1850-1920

When analysing changes in patterns of transport, it is important to distinguish between development and growth. Development involves changes in the nature of a transport mode or in the service which it provides. Growth concerns the extension of an existing mode of transport and its associated services. Development is usually accompanied or followed by growth but growth may occur in the absence of significant development. So it was with the railways in Britain. It is possible, with the perspective of time, to distinguish in broad terms a phase of *development* which lasted from the opening of the Liverpool and Manchester Railway in 1830 until the completion of the main interregional lines in 1852.

After 1852 came the *predominant* phase of railways in Britain (Girard 1965) which lasted until the end of the First World War, in round decades from 1850 to 1920, and was characterized by growth rather than development. Contemporaries would not have noticed a marked change in railway affairs in 1852, for the network was already being extended in Lowland Britain and on the coalfields before primary routes were completed in Scotland and Wales. There were, of course, important technical developments on the railways between 1850 and 1920, particularly in passenger services, but they did not make significant differences to the pattern of extension of the network.

Fig. 4 shows that the extension of routes continued at only a slightly lessened pace until 1880 when 25 000 km had been built. Further extension to 32 700 km in 1920 was at a much slower rate than the growth in freight traffic, suggesting that there was adequate capacity to carry the freight coming forward through the nineteenth century.

The direction of railway growth was determined by the fragmentation of the railway system among 200 independent companies. Many of these companies owned no more than one route, but the eleven companies with over 80 route kilometres each soon came to control half the network. By 1920 amalgamations had reduced the number of companies to 110 with the 15 largest companies owning 84 per cent of the system. The largest company in 1865 (Sherrington 1928) had 2050 route kilometres and the tenth largest 475 km. In the context of ten-ton wagon loads, an average passenger journey of 16 km, and an estimated average freight journey of 53 km (Hawke 1970), the fragmentation of the network amongst companies was unlikely to have a serious effect on the growth of traffic, but it did influence the shape of the growing network.

The regulation of economic competition between railway companies in Britain by the Railway Act of 1844 made geographical competition more intensive. It was widely believed that competition between companies rather than detailed regulation was the best way to combat the inherent monopoly of the railway system. Attempts by financial entrepreneurs, notably George Hudson, to control a substantial part of the network came to grief in the courts. Parliament preferred inter-regional mergers to the consolidation of geographically compact companies. Amalgamations after 1850 were in fact influenced more by the relative commercial strength of the companies than by concern for the cheaper working of the railways. The nearest approach to a regional system was the Great Western Railway, as Brunel, its first engineer, intended. With broad-gauge subsidiaries this company linked London with South Wales, Bristol, and South West England, but rivals struck through the Welsh uplands to penetrate the South Wales coalfield and built a hilly but shorter alternative route through Exeter to Plymouth. The North Eastern Railway eventually achieved virtual monopoly between Hull and the Scottish border.

Elsewhere rival companies competed to build branch lines into coalfield and industrial areas and alternative routes through agricultural and upland regions, filling spaces between existing routes but serving relatively small populations per kilometre of track.

Between 1838 and 1852, for example, all railway traffic from the English Midlands, the North of England, and Scotland to London combined at Rugby and terminated at London Euston (Route A on Fig. 1). As early as 1835 a more direct route was proposed from London to York via Cambridge, Peterborough and Lincoln (partly along the route of the Roman Ermine Street, which had also been designed for rapid access to York). In the overriding interest of a direct route the eventual Great Northern line, completed in 1852, served Lincoln and Cambridge by branches. Western branches from the Great Northern tapped the lucrative coal traffic of the Yorkshire coalfield and eventually provided alternative services not only to York but also to Leeds, Bradford, and Sheffield. The Midland Railway, which owned the original route B between Rugby, York, and Leeds, built its own line to London St. Pancras in 1868 and to Manchester in 1867. In 1899 the Manchester, Sheffield, and Lincolnshire Railway, renamed the Great Central for the occasion, pushed a line 166 km south from Leicester to reach London St. Marylebone. Thus Manchester, Bradford, and Sheffield each had three alternative lines to London.

In Highland Britain the situation was exacerbated by extensive areas of unpopulated upland. Competition resulted in two lines from central Scotland to Aberdeen and the incongruous provision of two independent railway lines to the West of Scotland on either side of the thinly populated Strath Fillan. Only a relatively rich country with stable finances and low interest rates could have financed so much duplication of route.

Fig. 5 shows the effect of the extension of the railway network in Northern England. By 1860 competition amongst companies led to the provision of three intercity routes between Liverpool and Manchester and two lines between all other large cities except Hull. There were then four Pennine crossings completed and a denser network of lines in the rural lowlands of the east. By 1920 many more rural branch lines had been built, especially up the Pennine valleys. On the coalfields the extension of production, especially to the east of Leeds, Sheffield, and Nottingham, led to many rail links to individual mines. This coalfield was served by the Midland, Great Northern, Great Central, and Lancashire and Yorkshire railways. The routes of the relatively late Hull and Barnsely railway may be recognized by following the line running north-west out of Hull, and its branches in country already well served by longer-established rivals.

The number of routes and nodes rose fourfold between 1850 and 1920 (Table 1), leading to a proportionate increase in the cyclomatic number. The number of spur branch lines determined that the proportion of routes of possible routes (gamma index) and of circuits to possible circuits (alpha index) changed little between 1850 and 1920.

TABLE 1

	Waterways		Railways			
	1830	1840	1850	1860	1920	1974
km^2 per km track	27	57	14	9	6	11
000 pop. per km track	3	8	2	2	2	5
Nodes (edges)	104	26	164	285	725	213
Junctions (vertices)	95	25	99	207	423	133
Subgraphs	3	3	2	1	2	1
Cyclomatic no.	10	4	67	79	304	81
Alpha index (%)	5	4	35	19	36	31
Gamma index (%)	37	38	56	46	57	54

It is difficult to discuss the changes wrought by the railways on the economic geography of Britain because we can only speculate whether the country would have continued to rely on a further extension of inland waterways for freight and of coaching service for passengers of whether automobile transport would have developed sooner. The long-held thesis that railways played a fundamental role in the geographical shaping of the North American economy has been challenged by Fogel (1964) and Fishlow (1965), who support their case by detailed measurements and the application of modern economic theory. The methods of this 'new economic history' have been applied to railways in England and Wales by Hawke (1970), who concludes that the social savings attributable to railways, defined as the difference between the cost of railway services and the hypothetical cost of providing similar services in the absence of railways, amounted to about 10 per cent of the national income. The greatest contribution of railways, in his view, lay in the increased comfort of passenger travel. The second most important contribution was the increased facility and decreased cost of coal and mineral transport.

Railways certainly facilitate the urbanization which gathered momentum as the nineteenth century progressed. Urbanization is, however, essentially associated with industrialization and both processes were well under way in Britain by 1830. The effect of railways on the pattern of towns, as it developed during the nineteenth century, is clearer to distinguish.

The greater comfort of passenger travel provided by the railway helped to create modern tourism, enabling large number of people to travel relatively long distances within their short holidays. In 1841 the British coasts were virtually empty. Coastal settlements were mineral ports or fishing harbours, for, with the exception of Liverpool, the larger ports were as far up river as coastal vessels could sail. There were a few small resorts and Brighton already had a population of 47 000 when reached by the railway. There were 600 000 people living in the coastal towns of England and Wales of over 5000 population in 1841 (apart from Liverpool 286 000), comprising 4 per cent of the total population. By 1921 the total population of similar towns had grown to 9 per cent of the total. Some inland resorts grew during the railway age but few were created in the same way as Blackpool or Southport. The most successful coastal resorts, if growth be a criterion of success, lay within 100 km of London or the industrial cities of the coalfields, and it was not until the end of the nineteenth century that long interregional holiday journeys were undertaken by more than a minority of tourists.

Railways came too late to prevent the consolidation of the nascent concentrations of manufacturing industry in large industrial villages on water-power sites and near coal-pits on the Pennine flanks, in central Scotland, the West Midland plateaux, and the South Wales valleys. In the absence of cheap coal transport before the 1840s Leeds, Manchester, and Birmingham were already outstripping the older centres of their regions. When the railways were built they reinforced the canals in

favouring the development of valley centres for the later stages of manufacturing and for services. Higher towns and villages, initially out of
reach of the railway, tended to grow as specialized manufacturing
settlements. Railways fossilized the pattern of settlement that they
found rather than encouraging the spread of the new manufacturing
industries. The potential area for new manufacture was greatly enlarged
but the presence of rail communication did not counteract the advantages
of contact, industrial knowledge, and the availability of capital in pre-
existing centres.

The pricing policies of the railway companies in Britain had a con-
servative effect upon industrial location. Variable costs certainly increase
in some proportion to distance, but where fixed and terminal costs are,
or are accounted to be, large elements in the total costs of transport, the
length of the journey may not be very significant either to the supplier
or to the purchaser of the transport service. The graphical analysis of
networks is valuable in this respect, for emphasizing the numbers of
nodes and links rather than the distances along routes. The pricing
policies of nineteenth-century railway managers are revealed in evidence
to Royal Commissions and to Select Committees of Parliament and in
the records of disputes that came to court. Much of this evidence is
reviewed by Hawke (1970). He concludes that with the development of
the railway system, charges tended to move away from a relationship to
distance and towards considerations based on the perceived long-term
interests of the railway companies. The detailed costing of services was
difficult to undertake for relatively few operating statistics were collected.

The very multiplicity of rates ensured that, once established, charges
only changed slowly. The conventional charges for terminal facilities
hardly altered during the latter half of the nineteenth century. Managers
sought to charge what the traffic would bear, ensuring that rates covered
variable costs and the conventional terminal costs, and made as much
contribution as possible to fixed costs. They were often prepared to
accept minimum profits, or even short-term losses, in the development
of new traffic. They did not make the maximization of profits the sole
criterion of their pricing policy. Of equal, or greater importance in many
instances, was the desire of the companies to assist the trade of the
region which they served. In the light of the established economic thinking of their day which stressed the long-term benefits of competition,
railway managers frequently sought access for their customers to a variety
of suppliers and markets. This was achieved by minimizing or ignoring
the relative distances separating suppliers and their markets. As this policy
was adopted by most companies, the geography of transport cost in
Britain reflected less and less the real relative position of places. Transport

costs on the canals and early roads had been too high a proportion of the final price to the consumer to allow distances to be transformed in this fashion. In the railway age ports were no longer solely dependent on the trade of their immediate hinterland, and cross-hauls of goods and raw materials were facilitated. Railway pricing policies, spontaneously applied by companies operating in different parts of the country, tended to preserve and extend the opportunities for existing producers wherever they were located. Isolated and peripheral producers did not lack trade on account of their location alone. Changes in the location of industry during the later nineteenth century owed more to technical factors and to differences in managerial efficiency than to geographical factors associated with transport costs.

This contrasts with the situation on the European mainland and in North America where distances were greater and most firms established themselves after a recognizable pattern of railway transport charges had developed. Analyses of industrial location during the railway age which place considerable emphasis on transport costs, including those of Weber (1904) and his followers, have therefore rather less relevance to British than to continental industries.

Within Britain the railways widened the market for farmers' produce and gave them access to a wider and often better range of seeds, farm machinery, and fertilizers. New dairy-product and market-gardening regions developed at much greater distances from the large urban markets than hitherto. The effect of railways on marketing, as Christaller (1934) has pointed out, was to weaken the importance of lower-order central places—the small country towns. This was especially important in the crucial early phase when through traffic was being sought at the expense of way traffic and several older market centres were temporarily bypassed by the railways. The railway-linked market towns were able to provide the benefits of bulk transport and attracted business from stock fairs which had previously taken place in the open country along the drove routes. Droving itself was replaced by the railway transport of cattle and sheep to marts alongside the tracks.

Eventually the majority of villages were quite close to a railway connection, and the railways made a small but significant contribution to the range of rural employment. Local handicraft industries, quarries, and eventually medium-sized shops suffered severely from standardized manufactured products supplied from or purchased in industrial towns and larger market centres. The Welsh slate tiles which roof late-nineteenth-century houses all over Britain are the most eloquent visual reminder of the all-pervasive influence of the Victorian railway.

5 Road transport expands 1920-70

During the greater part of the railway age there were no road vehicles of comparable power to railway locomotives. Research on internal combustion engines was going on while the railways were spreading and in 1885 the first modern car was produced in Germany. The manufacture of motor vehicles, shaped like coaches but with rubber tyres and driven by internal combustion engines, spread from Germany to Britain in 1896 and the first motor bus appeared on the roads in 1898. In 1903 motor vehicles were licensed and given full freedom of circulation on British roads, but it was only after the First World War that road transport began to make a significant contribution to the British transport system. Although pioneer development work on the motor car took place in Germany, France, Britain, and North America, the modern road transport system first developed on a large scale in North America and was copied, rather tardily, in Europe.

By 1920 there were 187 000 private cars on British roads, 101 000 goods vehicles, and 88 000 vehicles in public transport. A flood of ex-army vehicles and army-trained drivers were establishing local and intercity lorry and bus services all over Britain. The road network was 288 000 km. During the railway age eighteenth-century lanes and farm tracks had been upgraded for local use. They were generally wide enough for farm carts to pass each other but had sharp bends and some single-track sectors. As this road network could be entered at virtually any point and was nine times as long as the railway network it was much better adapted to individual needs than the railway. Existing forms of road transport expanded and wholly new types of traffic were created.

During the railway age trams and buses had played a growing role in local journeys to work. The development of bus networks, reaching out from the large towns and conurbations, now enabled people to live further from their work. Car owners in particular enjoyed a much wider choice of residence in relation to workplace (or workplace in relation to their home) and could also follow a new life style of frequent weekend excursions over a radius of 100 km or more and much longer and more varied shopping and social visits within their immediate locality. New patterns of housing followed the development of road transport, first as ribbon development along main roads and later as compact housing estates located several kilometres away from the commercial centre of cities. In local traffic the delivery van was a considerable advance in efficiency on the horse and cart.

In intercity transport, long-distance coach services were revived using motor coaches, charging fares in the 1920s which were 30 per cent lower than rail fares and drawing away from the railways a whole class of passengers who set a relatively low money value on their time. Road goods services soon came to provide a faster, cheaper, and more reliable medium of transport for the majority of manufacturers and wholesale traders. Long-distance line hauls can be very rapid by rail, but the marshalling of the wagons, their transfer from long-distance to local trains, and the modal split to road vehicles at terminal goods stations meant that the slower intercity road lorry provided a faster door-to-door delivery service within a range of 350 km. Road services were particularly competitive within a radius of 120 km and on routes transverse to the main lines of the railways. It is important in this context to remember that the average length of haul of lower-value commodities on the railways in 1938 was 103 km, and of higher-value commodities 172 km (Smith 1949). Although railways provided some free warehousing services, the frequency and regularity of road deliveries often enabled traders and manufacturers to hold smaller stocks of goods at less capital cost to themselves.

The pricing policies of the railways have been described in Chapter 4 above. Fixed costs form a much lower component of total costs in road haulage since individual hauliers do not need elaborate terminal and interchange facilities nor do they maintain a private track. It is therefore easier for a road haulier to calculate the true costs of the services he performs and to relate charges to these costs. Road transport offered a cheaper service for high-value goods on the more heavily used routes than the railway but was under no corresponding obligation to carry all goods offered to any destination. The operations of many manufacturing firms were of a suitable size to justify a small fleet of road vehicles under their own managements.

The rapid growth of road transport was facilitated by, and itself facilitated, developments in other sectors of the economy. The production of consumer durable goods for the home market became increasingly important, but exports of textiles, iron and steel goods, and coal declined. New firms manufacturing cars, machine tools, and the smaller consumer durables located themselves in South East England and the English Midlands while employment declined in South Wales, the southern Pennines, and Scotland—the outer manufacturing zones which had dominated the British economy during the canal and railway ages. Total employment in manufacturing industry remained stable but agriculture and mining employment declined steeply. The increase in total employment was absorbed by such service industries as banking, wholesale and retail trade, catering, and the professions. Thus towns grew partly at the expense of rural areas, large service centres developed more rapidly than small ones, and the increased population and wealth of Britain accumulated in the Midlands and South of England.

Road transport grew rapidly after 1920, halting only during the Second World War. The number of private cars reached one million in 1930 and 13 million (one per 4·3 people) in 1972. Private car vehicle kilometres (estimated) accounted for 77 per cent of all passenger kilometres travelled in Britain in 1972. The tramways reached their maximum extent in 1928 but then began to be replaced by buses. The last major fleet of tramcars was scrapped in 1962. Bus services expanded rapidly during the interwar years and accounted for 39 per cent of passenger kilometres in 1954 before declining (to 13 per cent in 1972) in face of rising car ownership. Traffic carried by road goods vehicles grew until it equalled that on the railways in 1955. In 1971 the roads carried 83 668 million ton kilometres of goods, 63 per cent of the total freight movement.

As the volume of road traffic increased it soon surpassed the capacity of the existing road network to carry it at optimum speeds and the newly created Ministry of Transport (1920) had to decide whether to fit the roads to the traffic or to try to fit the traffic to the roads. Initially 37 000 km of the road network were designated as 'main traffic arteries' and some financial aid was given to the local authorities responsible for their upkeep. A further 24 000 km qualified for a lower rate of national subsidy. This network was adequate in length to meet major intercity needs according to the criteria shown in Fig. 1. In 1930 100 000 km of 'classified' roads became the sole responsibility of the county councils and in 1936 the Ministry of Transport itself assumed responsibility for 7600 km of 'national trunk' roads and in 1948 for a further 6000 km.

The capacity of the trunk road network varied considerably from place to place and the improvement of the roads made slow progress. National schemes were published in 1924, 1929, and 1939 but the economic depression and the Second World War prevented most of the projects being carried out. Although the road network was virtually ubiquitous, traffic flows were highly concentrated. A postwar survey showed that 25 per cent of the traffic in Great Britain was flowing over 1 per cent of the road length and that 10 per cent of the road length (about 32 000 km) carried 66 per cent of the traffic. Most of the limited sums available for road improvement were spent on the widening of bottlenecks where major traffic flows were trying to squeeze themselves over narrow bridges or through the medieval street layout of market towns with serious loss of speed and danger of accident. For the greater part of the period British roads appear to have been the most crowded in the world with 41 vehicles per kilometre in 1971.

The body of geographical theory relating to roads (and to ports; see Chapter 6) is not great, but as early as 1929 Reilly (1929) had suggested that flows of local trade and traffic between places were proportional to the product of the population of the places and inversely proportional to the square of the distance between them in very much the same way as masses exercise mutual attraction in the Newtonian theory of gravitation. Although such simple gravity models have been found inadequate to explain the full complexity of traffic movement, they suggest that, as towns grow, new traffic generated is unlikely to flow evenly over a transport network inherited from a former age. In 1928 the first intercity motorway reserved for through traffic and partially isolated from the local road network was begun in Germany. Between 1933 and 1945 the German government planned and built a network of 2100 km of motorways.

Motorways were introduced to Britain in 1957 in order to provide increased capacity on the road network between industrial centres. The traffic capacity of a four-lane highway is three times that of a two-lane road: a further increase in the number of lanes gives a more than proportionate increase in capacity. The limitation of access to the highway increases capacity further by allowing higher speeds. The original motorway net linked London with the West Midlands, Merseyside (Route A on Fig. 1), and West Yorkshire (B). Later motorways linked London with South Wales (D), the West Midlands with South West England and South Wales (J, K), Liverpool with West Yorkshire (M), Edinburgh with Clydeside (F). Major trunk routes comprising four-lane highways including short motorway stretches have been built from London to North East England, London to the south coast ports, and from Lancashire to Clydeside (E).

As the first 1600 km of motorway in Britain were nearing completion new criteria were being established for motorway routes (Ministry of Transport 1970). Priority for industrial freight traffic has been replaced by the aim of general accessibility expressed as an intention to bring motorways to within 16 km of all towns of 80 000 or more by 1990. Connectivity will be greatly increased, sea and airports will be linked to the system, and historic towns will be freed from heavy through traffic. These objectives are to be achieved by building a further 3500 km of motorways and four-lane highways and a further 2900 km of improved trunk roads, thus doubling the capacity of the road system during a period when road traffic is expected to rise by only 70 per cent. The current plans are based on sophisticated predictions of car ownership

and of the extent to which motorways generate new traffic by their very
existence. Interaction models based on comprehensive traffic surveys
have been related to the proposals of Regional Economic Planning
Councils for the location of new towns, industrial estates, and ports.
The proposals provide for a much lower density of motorways in relation
to population and area than those of West Germany and the Netherlands.

Figure 6 shows how motorways and four lane highways compare with
railway routes in Northern England. The M62 (the motorway version of
Route M Fig. 1) skirts the chief towns, which have spur links to it.
Lancashire, where the first section of British motorway was opened in
1958, shows a nascent network of urban motorways. Only the West
Midlands, among other British conurbations, is likely to achieve a similar
network this century.

The improvement in accessibility may be measured in several ways.
Table 2 takes time as a measure, comparing journey times in 1974 by
road, road and motorway (where available), and by passenger train. It is
not based on measurement as a traffic survey would be, but transforms
distance into time on the assumption that vehicles travel on ordinary
roads at an average speed of 50 k.p.h. and on motorways at an average
of 80 k.p.h. Travellers by road can set off at any time. On the railway
they have to wait for the train. In order to make the railway journey
times comparable with those on road, the average waiting time between
trains (half the average interval between trains departing between 08.00
and 18.00 hours) has been added to the rail journeys. Over these relatively
short distances (Liverpool is 206 km from Hull) the motorway provides
the fastest route, although if passengers begin their journeys shortly
before a train is about to depart there is little difference between the two
modes. From the comparison, summation or multiplication of matrices
such as Table 2 more detailed indices of the relative accessibility of
places or of the general accessibility within regions may be obtained.

TABLE 2
Journey times across the Pennines 1974

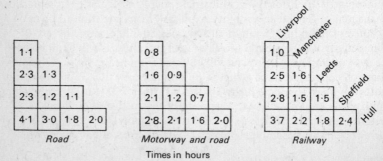

Road

Motorway and road

Railway

Times in hours

RAILWAYS

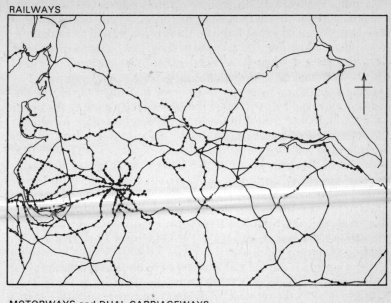

MOTORWAYS and DUAL CARRIAGEWAYS

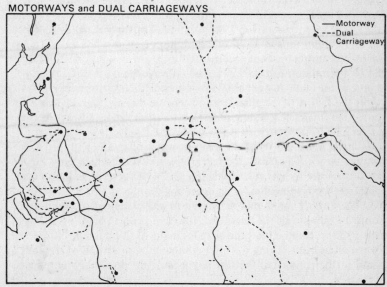

Fig. 6. Northern England: railways and motorways 1974

As in the 1920s and 1930s, the new highway scheme has been delayed by capital cuts due to recurrent economic crises. At any one time almost 80 per cent of capital expenditure on roads is committed to work in progress so that substantive cuts in the road budget can only be made by postponing planned schemes. A further major brake on trunk road construction in Britain, as in Western Europe generally, has beeen the strength of opposition by people living in the immediate vicinity of the proposed route and by nationally organized amenity groups. The building of the M4 motorway from London to South Wales was delayed while such objectors exercised their rights under planning legislation to dispute the route to be followed across the Wiltshire Downs. In urban areas the higher cost of the motorways (2·5 to 3 times as great as that of motorways between cities), disruption during construction, permanent loss of housing, and the increase in noise and pollution led to each scheme being subjected to exhaustive, expensive, and protracted inquiries. The London urban road plan, which proposed a series of concentric motorways, first proposed in 1964, was abandoned in 1973 after over £1 million had been spent on major inquiries.

The competition of road transport began to be felt by the railways between the wars. Railways were in financial difficulties by the late 1920s and in 1928 the route network began to contract. Route length fell by 740 km (2 per cent) during the period 1928—48, and by a further 3400 km (11 per cent) from 1948 to 1962. Traffic (Fig. 4) declined from 343 million tons in 1923 to 266 million tons in 1938 and, after a brief revival during postwar reconstruction, from 289 million tons in 1953 to 196 million tons in 1971. The railways found it difficult to respond to the changing economic fortunes of their customers.

Ater the failure of a modernization scheme during the mid-1950s to improve the financial standing of the now nationalized railway company the Beeching Report (British Railways Broad 1963) drew attention to the financial implications of the concentration of traffic within the railway network. The least-used half of the network, which only carried 5 per cent of the freight ton kilometres and 4 per cent of the passenger kilometres, was responsible for an operating deficit of £20 million in 1962. The Report concluded that revenue was sufficient to cover costs on only 14 000 km of the network. A further report (British Railways Board 1965) recommended the abandonment of duplicated routes between cities built during the inter-company competition of the railway age and further suggested that the network might profitably be reduced to 4800 km.

Following these Reports 7800 km of railway were abandoned in 1963—9 inclusive, not without protest from many of the areas which lost railway service, bringing the network down to 20 000 km.

A comparison of Figs. 5 and 6 shows the changes in the railway network between 1920 and 1974 in part of Northern England. Table 1 gives data based on the maps. Although the network was halved, only thinly populated rural areas in Lincolnshire, the York Wolds, and the Pennines were significantly further away from railway services. The alpha and gamma indices show little change so that, in a topological sense, the loss of efficiency was minimal. On Fig. 6 all passenger stations are shown, illustrating the difference between the three types of passenger service now provided. On the intercity lines from London to Scotland most stations have been closed in order to speed long distance passenger and freight trains. Rural branch lines served by diesel car units, on the other hand, retain a high frequency of stations as do the commuter services into Manchester and Liverpool.

Railways continued to enjoy technical advantages over road haulage in the long distance carriage of bulk freight on line haul and in the movement of large numbers of passengers in urban areas. It is arguable that motor buses on reserved track could carry urban passengers more efficiently than can railways but Britain has not yet felt able to devote sufficient capital resources into transport to enable the abandonment of existing and serviceable systems in favour of costly new systems which might be more efficient in the long run.

The railways faced formidable problems in developing a specialized ancillary network for specific traffic movements out of a network built to carry virtually all the traffic to all the places. The slow decline of their traffic left the railways without the financial resources to redevelop their system while successive governments lacked the confidence, and often the means, to offer sufficiently massive state investment.

Nevertheless some services were developed. In particular, passenger services in the London area expanded (explaining the increase in total passenger business shown during the 1930s in Fig. 4). South of the Thames electrification of track combined with attractive season ticket rates to encourage London workers to leave the inner suburbs, served by rival trams and buses, for new homes in Surrey, Kent, and even Sussex. North of the Thames underground railways emerged on the surface encouraging extensive dormitory settlement to distances of 10 to 20 km from the inner city. Railways fostered and benefited from the outward spread of large cities where the scale of the development generated sufficient density of traffic.

Intercity electrification was postponed until 1954 when the Sheffield to Manchester line was electrified primarily for freight transport. The electric system of South East England reached the Channel Ports in 1962 and Bournemouth in 1967 while the route from London to Lancashire (Route A on Fig. 1) was electrified in 1966 and from

Lancashire to Glasgow (Route E) in 1974. This brought the electrified track of British railways to 4500 km, 23 per cent of the total which compared with 32 per cent in West Germany and 27 per cent in France. After the replacement of steam traction by diesel electric engines on the rest of the system by 1967 many intercity passenger services were improved since market research showed that each per cent decrease in journey time led to about one per cent increase in passenger traffic, and the electrification of services between London, Birmingham, Manchester, and Liverpool had encouraged a substantial number of air passengers to return to the railways.

Inland waterways, like railways, suffered a substantial decline in traffic as road transport developed. Traffic fell to 5·5 million tons in 1971 (excluding the Manchester Ship Canal). By the 1950s commercial traffic was concentrated on the river navigations focusing on London and the Humber, some of which had been improved to take larger craft. Of 3200 km of waterways under the control of the Waterways Board 1000 km was regarded as having no commercial future.

It is almost a paradox in transport geography that the improvement of particular accessibility between specific points usually leads to additions to the route system and a dispersion of traffic flow along the new routes. The improvement of general accessibility, however, is often associated with the concentration of traffic flows into certain routes of a network. The most economic way to improve general accessibility is often found to be the construction of high capacity routes whose initial cost, it is hoped, will be balanced by economies of scale for transport users. Where transport modes are in competition, each mode may decide to develop high capacity on parallel routes: the simultaneous construction of a motorway and an electrified railway from London to Carlisle (Route AE in Fig. 1) during the 1960s is a good example of this. The avoidance of competition by the integration of modes poses the problem as to which should receive the investment. This issue is raised in Chapter 7 but first it is necessary to review the development of the intermodal nodes of the British transport system.

6 Ports

The nodes of the British transport system include, in addition to the road, rail, and canal interchanges mentioned in previous chapters, ports where land transport meets sea and air transport. Only a small proportion of the many natural harbours and anchorages of the British coastline have ever been used as seaports. Similarly only 33 airfields have developed commercial traffic, and only 4 handled more than 5 per cent of British passenger traffic in 1972. The conditions for successful port development are fairly restrictive. The initial location of a port depends on the geography of supply areas and markets and on the development of the cheapest and/ or most expeditious routes between them. This demand may arise from inland or overseas traffic. Once built, sea and airports may, in the absence of natural or man-made obstacles to further expansion, attract industrial and warehouse facilities and so themselves generate a proportion of their own growth traffic. Otherwise growth of port traffic must either be sustained by growth in the original trades for which it was established or by the development of new technical facilities at the port which attract traffic from other routes. Changes in the design and size of vehicles have been the leading factors in changing port technology. As traffic has expanded, larger and more complex ships and aircraft have been developed in order to benefit by economies of scale. Larger ships require longer quays and a greater depth of water alongside; larger aircraft need longer runways. Both demand faster turnround. The response of British ports to changing ship technology is extensively discussed by Bird (1963, 1971) and Couper (1972). Sealy (1957) describes airport development.

During the canal era, improved inland distribution fostered a growth of trade at the ports. Stone quays replaced wooden piers and the first docks were excavated in the larger ports. As coalmining expanded new ports were built as close to the pits as possible. Seaham (1823), West Hartlepool (1847), Port Clarence (1834), and Middlesbrough (1830) exemplify this process in the North East of England. Rival coal-owners occasionally constructed rival ports as at Hartlepool and West Hartlepool, Cardiff and Barry.

During the railway age, the cost of land transport within Britain declined but there was a marked development of export trade, and the railways, by improving transport links with the hinterland, further encouraged the growth of existing ports and the proliferation of new ones. Competition between railway companies led to the development of rival ports for coal (including Goole, Hull, and Immingham on the Humber estuary) and for short sea crossings. Traffic for Ireland passed through the old ports of Glasgow, Liverpool, and Bristol but also through new railway ports built on peninsulas or sheltered bays at Ardrossan, Stranraer, Barrow, Heysham, Fleetwood, Holyhead, and Milford Haven. There was a similar variety of cross-channel services to Europe. Because the railways dominated the internal traffic of Britain so completely between 1850 and 1920 and because there were serious capital shortages during the interwar years, the pattern of ports and traffic which had been established during the first three decades of the railway age was not greatly changed until the latter half of the twentieth century.

The volume of trade at British ports, as estimated by Imlah and others (Mitchell and Deane 1971), rose slowly during the early part of the nineteenth century, doubling between 1800 and 1830 and then doubling about every twenty years subsequently (that is by 1850, 1867, 1887, and 1913). During the interwar years the volume of imports rose by 30 per cent but there was no significant change in the volume of exports. The volume of trade rose from 115 million tons in 1938 to 247 million tons in 1971. This increase was almost entirely due to increased oil traffic.

The increase in traffic meant much more work for the ports. During the first half of the nineteenth century the size of vessels was limited by their wooden construction and sail spread. The average vessel in European and coastal trade was 100 tons, and a smaller number of vessels of 250 tons and upwards traded to North America and the Far East. The increased trade required more ships to carry it and it was necessary to extend dock and harbour facilities. In particular small wet docks were built in the large estuarine ports.

During this time steamships were developed experimentally, although the age of steam at sea is roughly equivalent to the railway age on land and it was only in 1883 that the registered tonnage of British steamers first exceeded that of sailing ships. Steam was first used to increase the speed of journeys. Steamboats were crossing the Clyde in 1812 and the North Atlantic in 1833 but the bulk of their fuel and the weight of their engines left relatively little commercial cargo space available. It was only with the coming of the iron (later steel) hull that it was possible to apply the general principle that the cargo capacity of a steamship increases in cubic ratio to its dimensions, but that the power of the engines need only be increased as the square of those dimensions. In 1838, for instance, I. K. Brunel built the wooden paddle steamer *Great Western* to link his London to Bristol railway with New York. She was by far the largest ship of her day at 1340 GRT. Only twenty years later he built the iron-hulled

Great Eastern of 18 900 GRT. In coastal waters the first iron collier was brought into service in 1850. During the second half of the nineteenth century, there was a rapid expansion in the size and cargo-carrying capacity of ships associated with major technical improvements in ships' engines. Although improved marine engineering knowledge enabled sailing ships of 5000 tons to be built for bulk trades like grain, steamships of comparable dimensions could carry four times as many tonkilometres per annum as sailing vessels by the end of the century. Further, in 1869 the opening of the Suez Canal revolutionized the geography of world sea trade by halving the length of the sea passage to India along a route which only steamships could profitably use.

Thus the increased carrying capacity of ships freed ports from the need to extend their facilities in direct proportion to the growth in the volume of trade. The increased capital cost of the larger ships, however, caused owners to press for faster turnround in port. For this purpose specialized unloading and warehousing facilities were constructed for each main traffic.

The many ports which had been established during the development of coalfields and railways retained their specialist functions, but much of the increased general cargo was handled in the larger estuarine ports. These ports were already attracting new industry to bolster their trade and were in a better position to raise capital for the dredging of deep-water channels and the construction of elaborate wet-dock systems, enabling ships to load and discharge cargoes at all states of the tide. The need for direct rail access to the births led to the construction of complex systems of branching docks, generally located between the original port and the mouth of the estuary, to give the longest possible rail-ship interface within the restricted area of the port.

In addition to the provision of specialized facilities, the larger estuarine ports established commodity exchanges and other commercial facilities, often housing the headquarter office of the shipping companies which served them.

During the eighteenth century London handled three-quarters of British overseas trade. The development of trade in textiles and metal goods during the canal era encouraged the growth of trade in Bristol, Liverpool, Glasgow, and Hull. These ports became the chief provincial centres of British overseas trade during the railway age, collecting 32 per cent of customs revenue in 1843 when London received 55 per cent. A new port was built at Manchester in 1894 on the completion of the 57-km Manchester Ship Canal for seagoing vessels. This development followed the pattern at Glasgow during the eighteenth century in providing for the inland penetration of sea transport into a rapidly expanding trading area.

Several schemes designed to develop the potential of the many deep-water harbours on the western coasts of Britain to provide rapid rail-sea transit between Europe and North America came to nothing, for shippers preferred the frequent regular sailings and the warehousing facilities of the established ports of the English lowlands and the North Sea coast of Europe. So the bulk of the Irish emigrants travelled to the New World through Liverpool as did substantial numbers of the Scandinavian emigrants of the later nineteenth century.

Fig. 7 illustrates the concentration of traffic which has taken place during the last century from the coal trade. The squares represent the tonnage shipped out of each port in domestic and export trade. The virtual disappearance of coal exports, which amounted to 12 million tons in 1872, reduced the total tonnage handled from 20 million tons in 1872 to 7 million tons in 1972. The proportion of the traffic handled in Newcastle, the largest port in the trade, remained the same, the number of ports handling more than 1 per cent of the total trade fell from 21 to 10. By 1972 only one port was handling the trade of each coalfield outside North East England.

The development of road transport was slow to alter the relative distribution of port facilities and trade in Britain. Investment money was hard to come by and port development had a low priority among Government reconstruction projects. The larger ports were owned by public trusts and many medium-sized ports by the railways, who had larger modernization problems on their own routes. The plans for the first 1600 km of motorways envisaged no direct motorway links to ports. With ageing equipment went a system of labour relations and practices which compared unfavourably in productivity with that of major ports on the European mainland.

The first scheduled air services from Britain flew to Paris and to Brussels in 1929, carrying mail and a small payload of passengers. Inter-war air traffic developed to cater for urgent passengers and surcharged mail so that London remained not only as the focal point of the network but also the preponderant point of origin of the traffic. Short internal air routes were in operation by 1934 when the Post Office granted the first internal mail contract from Scotland to the Orkney Islands. A network of air services linking the larger British towns existed by 1935.

London retained its pre-eminent position when air services resumed after the Second World War. In 1972, for example 71 per cent of the domestic and internal passengers passed through the London airports (including Luton). This nodal position reflects the predominance of external (77 per cent) over domestic flights and also the position of London at the surface communications hub of the South East and

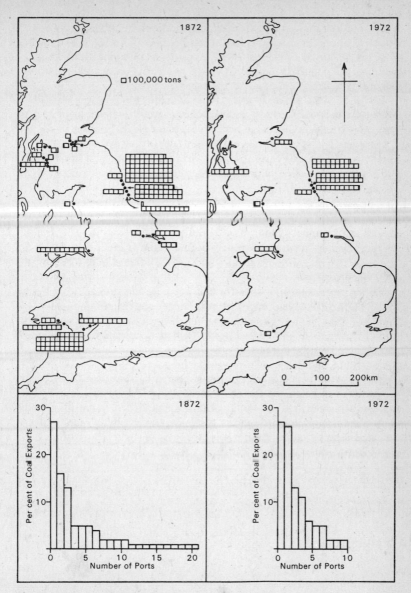

Fig. 7. Coal loadings 1872 and 1972. Based on *Brown's Export List* (1872) and National Ports Council (1972).

Midlands of England, which house many of the industries providing air freight and the majority of wealthy and moderately wealthy people in Britain. London has an important strategic position in the world network of air routes as one of the 'gateway' airports into Europe from North America, the chief load centre of world air traffic, and handles more passengers than any other airport outside the U.S.A.

British internal services have not expanded as fast as those abroad and traffic between London and Manchester experienced a notable set-back when train services were accelerated after electrification of the line in 1966. Air transport can only offer limited advantages of speed in relation to the cost of passenger fares over land journeys of less than 300 km, and only the London to Newcastle and Scotland routes exceed this distance on the British mainland.

Air transport has proved popular over routes involving short sea crossings so that 11 British provincial airports have direct services to Ireland, the Channel Islands, and to European resorts during the holiday season. The rural air transport services in Britain, from Glasgow and Inverness to Kintyre, the Hebrides, Orkneys, and Shetlands also obviate short sea crossings.

Britain has a wealth of sites for sites for harbours and airfields but the technological development of both feeder routes and line-haul vehicles during the last two centuries has favoured increasing concentration of traffic through selected ports. This tendency has been partially counteracted by the interest of cities and regions in retaining a share of the traffic through their own ports. As the government has assumed increasing control of major capital investment it has been presented with the problem of balancing the optimum port system for the country (if this can be agreed) against the individual demands for economic development from its component regions. Some help in resolving such conflicts may be found by considering the future role of each port within a possible integrated national transport system.

7 Towards integrated transport systems

The evolution of transport in Britain has been characterized by short recurrent periods of competition during which new transport media have developed rapidly, creating much new traffic and partially replacing the services and networks of older media. Specialized and/or supplementary transport services continued to run on the remaining network of the older media. In the early 1960s it looked as if road transport would dominate the network of the second half of the twentieth century as thoroughly as railways had dominated in the later nineteenth century. Indeed the 'stage' of road transport *predominance* had already been reached in North America, which is the source area of most twentieth-century innovation and change.

In Western Europe five largely independent factors, which may be characterized as spatial, cultural, conceptual, technological, and financial, have converged to divert the apparently inevitable future of road dominance into the prospect of transport integration.

Densities of population, roads, railways, and traffic in Britain are among the highest in the world, so the space for new transport routes and nodes was becoming limited and expensive. The loss of agricultural land to the intercity motorway programme made no serious inroads on farming productivity but urban motorways involved the destruction of large swathes of property. The London urban ring road proposals, for instance, with their numerous junctions, involved the removal of 15 000 houses. Ports must be redesigned in order to handle container traffic efficiently. The proposed new airport at Maplin, with its associated aircraft maintenance hangars, offices, and access roads, would have required 80 km² of land.

All new transport media change the *cultural* landscape to some extent. The spread of car ownership and the consequent demand for a higher-capacity road system threatened to metamorphose city centres and towns and to destroy the attractiveness of cultural centres and tourist areas by the very process of making them accessible to hundreds or thousands of private cars at once. In North America some cities and suburbs were built to the specification of one or two cars per family. To rehouse the population of Britain at the density of the Los Angeles conurbation, however, would put 80 700 km² (equivalent to 65 per cent of the present agricultural land) under urban land use.

The multiple pressures on land in Britain and the need to control the complex flows of traffic in American cities popularized the *concept* of the planned local or even regional environment and stimulated the adaptation of planning techniques to deal with traffic and land-use problems. The development of computing systems, which first became available to planners during the 1950s, enabled the actual and potential movements of traffic, the desire lines of potential travellers, and the complex interactions of changes in patters of land use and traffic flow to be programmed. Elaborate traffic and land-use surveys, which were carried out in many American and British cities during the 1960s, demonstrated the interdependence of homes, shops, offices, workplaces, and traffic flow patterns. They also showed the relative suitability of different transport media for varying densities and directions of traffic.

Transport *technologists* turned their attention to the weakest points in transport systems—the nodes where feeder-distributor vehicles transfer their cargo to or from the long-haul carriers. It is inherently difficult to balance the trickle of feeder-distributor traffic, which may be semi-continuous, with the intermittent bulk movement of the line-haul vehicle. The problem may be partially solved if the cargo is packed in units which are portable by the smallest feeder-distributor vehicle and can be quickly stacked together to provide an adequate cargo for the bulk vehicle. Lorries and their cargoes fulfill this condition when using roll-on roll-off ferries; otherwise rigid rectangular containers may be used. Containers were first used on British railways in 1926 to convey furniture and other miscellaneous small cargoes from consignor by lorry, rail flat car, and lorry to the consignee. The large-scale containerization of cargo developed first in North American coastal traffic during the the 1950s and was tested in the supply of war material to Vietnam during the 1960s. Such large-scale container operations involve the installation of special equipment at each node served. Special cranes and radical changes in the layout of cargo-handling facilities are necessary at sea- and airports. Although containers can be carried on existing vehicles and vessels, a fully efficient operation requires purpose-built ships and railway rolling stock. In such a system the container can take advantage, on the different stages of its journey, of the ubiquity of the road network, the cheapness and speed of railway on long overland hauls, the speed of air transport, and the low cost of sea transport. Containerization can only repay its heavy capital costs and provide an improved transport service when the transport media integrate their operations.

Containers came into use more rapidly in Britain than in other West European countries. Freightliner container services began on the railways in 1965. The 1968 Transport Act allowed the National Freight Corporation

absorbed into new policy for railways in 1974, an 18 000 km railway
network was retained. The withdrawal of further services required
consultation with relevant planning authorities. Limited subsidies wer[e]
also provided for bus routes, and local district councils were allowed t[o]
operate and subsidize bus services in their area. Money was also forth-
coming for experimental minibus and combined postal-passenger
services.

Forward projections of the growth of air traffic suggested, in 1957[,]
that the London airports at Heathrow and Gatwick would reach their
capacity during the 1980s. It was believed that the projected increase
in aircraft movements made a third airport preferable to expansion at
Heathrow and Gatwick. There was additionally a formidable lobby of
objectors to increased aircraft movement over the western and southe[rn]
suburbs of London. Each proposal for the site of a third airport raise[d]
similar storm of local opposition. After 17 years of public discussion,
the prospect of larger aircraft and much higher fuel costs suggested a
downward revision of estimates of future aircraft movement. The doc[u]
mentation of the discussion includes the Roskill Report (1971) which
at a cost of £1·2 million for the associated inquiries and research, con[-]
tains a very thorough analysis of the issues involved. Out of the contr[o]
versy came demands for a national airport policy and suggestions for [a]
wider distribution of international air services to regional capitals in
Britain. Such services might draw custom from wider hinterlands, new[ly]
made accessible by the motorway and intercity rail networks which h[ad]
been brought into being while the debate over London's third airport
was in progress.

At seaports two technical developments, the increase in size of vess[els]
and containerization, favoured the concentration of new installations
into a few deep-water terminals. The improvement of accessibility by
land potentially reinforced the tendency towards further concentrati[on]
of trade. On the other hand the commercial and industrial interests of
existing ports were deeply entrenched. The Rochdale Report (1962)
favoured the concentration of British trade, with most emphasis, follo[w]
ing changing patterns of British trade, on development of North Sea a[nd]
English Channel ports and least further development of Bristol,
Manchester, and Glasgow. Investment in ports amounted to £220 mill[ion]
between 1965 and 1969 but development did not proceed exactly
according to Rochdale or the later National Ports Development Coun[cil]
proposals. Government control of investment was initially limited to
schemes of over £500 000. After the refusal of a major development
scheme for Bristol in 1966 governments have hesitated to condemn
major schemes of individual ports in principle. Subsequent financial

which owns road vehicles and depots, to operate, through a subsidiary
company, container-carrying trains between the major conurbations as
well as company trains circulating between the individual factories and
warehouses of a firm in different parts of the country. Unitized traffic
grew from 6 million tons in 1967 to 22 million tons in 1972, of which
47 per cent was roll-on roll-off and 53 per cent container.

Capital investment in trunk roads, railway and port modernization,
new aircraft, containers, pipelines, ships, and the electricity supergrid
strained the *financial* resources of all transport companies. Many operators, including port trusts, railway companies, and airlines, were unable
to renew their equipment or to invest in new and technically superior
installations, without government help. There was a long tradition of
subsidies to the sea and air companies which carried mail. Government
subsidies for the upkeep of roads have been described in Chapter 5. By
the 1960s the state was deeply involved in the building of motorways
and estuary bridges, and other transport operators were calling for
government aid to finance their investment and maintenance programmes.
In publishing their replies to these requests governments gave some in-
formation on the relative costs and benefits of investment in different
transport media. During the rather frequent periods of financial retrench-
ment after 1955 it became increasingly difficult to justify investment in
competitive transport facilities. By the 1970s there was further competition for the limited capital funds from three major new projects: the
Channel Tunnel, Concorde, and London's Third Airport.

It would be a serious oversimplification to suggest that government
spending decisions were only influenced by a search for over-all
efficiency in the British transport services. The protracted public debates,
however, did much to inform influential opinion about the technical
issues involved.

The integration of transport media began at the pressure points of
the system. These were the central areas of cities, remote rural districts,
and nodes subjected to the rapid growth of traffic. Integration was
advocated by the Royal Commission on Transport in 1930, and following its recommendations the London Passenger Transport Board was set
up in 1933. It was not until the 1968 Transport Act that five further
conurbation transport authorities were established. These authorities
received capital grants from state funds to build interchanges between
existing bus and railway services and, in some conurbations, to construct
underground railways.

The costs of providing land for new transport facilities rose rapidly.
As long-term planning is cheaper than misplaced investment the integration of transport was helped by the further sophistication of gravity

models and by the application of cost-benefit analysis. Estimates were attempted of the total social cost of schemes, that is the cost of the change in transport facilities plus the costs arising from associated change in complementary transport media, land-use patterns, and the quality of life for people living in the vicinity. The quality of other people's lives is difficult to measure in any objective way but the attempt to quantify a large number of dissimilar factors has led to clearer analytical thinking about transport investment.

The development of integrated transport planning has been associated with more elaborate attempts to forecast demand for transport. Reasons of spatial efficiency (including the simple alpha and gamma indices mentioned in Chapter 2) and accessibility help to explain the adequacy of a network to accommodate an existing situation or trend, the growth of road transport for instance. If it is thought desirable to make a major change in the scale of road transport provision, both the immediate and the consequential costs and benefits must be carefully considered. Planners must estimate future trends in the demand for transport and also try to envisage the transport system which will give the best service to the economy, relative to its cost, during the near and medium future. Planners are, in fact, often restricted to suggesting additions to the present transport system which will make the best use of the limited funds available to them. In the planning of major nodes such as sea- and airports it is necessary to consider the amount of employment they will create and the consequent demand for housing and other services near their proposed location. Alternative locations for a node or paths for a route are usually available and must be evaluated.

Previous chapters have shown how nineteenth-century railway routes were planned on slender evidence of potential traffic and that the need for road widening of port expansion in the early twentieth century was related to the actual congestion of vehicles. Transport planners in the 1960s have tried to understand congestion through detailed research into the origin and destination of the vehicles concerned. Forecasts of congestion on routes or at nodes are made by extrapolating present trends in the growth of traffic, preferably in relation to expected growth of population, wealth, and propensity to travel. If the future demand for transport can be forecast in this way, it is better to consider how alternative routes, nodes, or modes would supply the expected demand rather than simply to enlarge the existing facilities. Complex forecasting exercise of this kind are particularly prudent where large capital investments are envisaged.

The gravity model was defined in Chapter 5 above as the observed propensity for interaction between places to increase in proportion to

the product of their populations and to decrease in proportion to the distance between them. If I_{ij} is the interaction between place i and place j; P_i and P_j are their respective populations; P_{ij} the distance between them; b an exponent of that distance, and k a constant, then:

$$I_{ij} = k \frac{P_i P_j}{d_{ij}{}^b}$$

This basic expression enables estimates to be made of the effect on traffic between specified places of several factors: change in their population or in the wealth of the population or in their propensity to travel; changes in the time or cost of travel, which may be substituted for distance (d) in the expression; changes in the demand and supply of commodities. The gravity model is applicable at different scales to journeys to work, to shopping trips, to intercity flows of goods or passengers, to long-distance air traffic, to tourist travel and to the delimitation of hinterlands. The simple gravity model must, however, be modified for the study of each type of interaction and calibrated (a function of the constant k) to known traffic flows by empirical studies. Readers are referred to Taafe and Gauthier (1973), Hay (1973), and Haggett (1965) for details of the necessary elaborations to suit each case. The principle modifications lie in the distance exponent (b) which varies considerably with mode of transport and with type of traffic, in complementarity—the extent to which the interacting places have specialized on complementing functions—and, in the case of two places at some distance from each other, in the chance that a third intermediate place will provide an 'intervening opportunity' to obtain the good or service for which the journeys are undertaken.

Three examples are given below to illustrate recent developments in transport integration in Britain. In its consideration of rural transport the Beeching Report (British Railways Board 1963) considered that the closure of rural railway lines would reduce railway costs substantially without losing much revenue. Further studies suggested that no public transport system could show a profit in many rural areas. The loss of rail services which had provided an integral part of rural economy for over a century seemed likely to lead to individual distress, further depopulation, and an end to any hope of diversifying the employment structure of extensive areas of Scotland, Wales, and the North and West of England. The 1968 Transport Act therefore provided state subsidies for the operation of specific 'socially necessary' railway services, including rural branch lines, and the retention of intermediate stations on express intercity routes. With these subsidies, annually renewed until they were restrictions on investment have not been applied selectively in furtherance of a national policy. Meanwhile 8 major general cargo ports have been equipped for deep-sea and 11 for short-sea container ships. The private port of Felixstowe has increased trade from 50 000 tons per annum in the 1960s to 2·2 million tons in 1970.

The reconstruction of railway finance under the 1968 Transport Act was based on a realistic assessment of their limited role in intercity freight and passenger traffic. For the first time intercity transport was seen as a system of complementary media and quantity licensing of road goods transport was proposed in order to direct on to the railway the bulk of goods travelling over 160 km and in vehicles of over 16 tons. It was then believed that, given a predicted national growth rate of 3·5 per cent per annum the railways would be able to cover their costs and finance their investment from revenues during the 1970s. The limitations on road goods transport were never imposed and the national economy failed to grow at a rate of 3·5 per cent so British Rail was in deficit again by 1972. By 1973 British Rail had ceased to believe in the possibility of a commercially viable network of any length and asked for treatment as a social service on the ground that it would cost more to close the system and provide alternative road facilities than to keep it open. After feasibility studies of 7000 and 5000 km networks, the government agreed to retain the 18 000 km network. They also promised £900 million to pay for the electrification of a further 2000 km of intercity and commuter routes, the development of further track signalling and the installation of computer-controlled wagon movement systems. Although the oil crisis of 1974 caused a reduction of the railway investment programme, it reinforced arguments in favour of the use of electrified railways to carry a greater share of intercity transport. Similar considerations fortified the British and French governments in their decision in 1973 to build a Channel Tunnel from Calais to Dover and so funnel a greater proportion of the growing traffic between Britain and the European mainland through Kent.

It was suggested in Chapter 1 that the geography of Britain favours a rational provision of transport routes as outlined in Fig. 1 with additional feeder and distributor routes up to the desired density of coverage. The actual development of the network, as analysed in Chapters 2–6, has been influenced more by the level of decision-making, that is the power, responsibilities, and knowledge of the decision-makers, than by either the technology available or the environmental problems of building the routes. Accessibility has increased enormously whether measured as the time required to travel between particular places or as the variety of places which may be attained from any one starting-point by a comparable expenditure of money or effort. Most people in the 1770s could only travel as far as they could walk: in the 1970s most households have a private car. The canal improved particular accessibility in terms of cost rather than of time. The railway cut cost and time, extending its network to almost every village, opening up completely new dimensions of movement. Road transport improved general accessibility for the individual as much as the railway had done for the village and suburb. Further improvement in accessibility can only be achieved by large-scale investment. By refining and developing their concepts and by appreciating the variety of spatial conflicts involved, geographers can contribute to the discussion on how best to use the limited funds available to British transport.

Further reading

The most comprehensive outline of recent work on transport networks
is found in P. Haggett and R. J. Chorley (1969), although there is a more
limited treatment of the subject in P. Haggett (1965) and more recent
discussion in A. Hay (1973) and E. J. Taaffe and H. L. Gauthier (1973).
A valuable short introduction is provided by K. Briggs (1972). All those
sources include some of the work of K. J. Kansky (1963) and F. Horton
(ed.) (1968) which are not so widely obtainable in Britain. Several standard
textbooks on quantitative geography, notably J. P. Cole and C. A. M. King
(1968), contain chapters on network analysis.

The most comprehensive recent economic history of British transport,
with an excellent bibliography, is II. J. Dyos and D. H. Aldcroft (1969).
Other shorter general accounts include C. I. Savage (1966) and J. Simmons
(1962). Earlier publications to which all writers on transport history are
indebted include W. T. Jackman's classic (1916, reprinted 1962), and
E. A. Pratt (1912, reprinted 1970). There are valuable sections on transport in several standard economic histories of Britain, most notably in
J. H. Clapham (1926–38). The most comprehensive treatment of transport in an economic geography of Britain is found in W. Smith (1949,
reprinted 1968). In J. H. Appleton (1962) there is a unique study of the
role of the land surface and other pre-existing elements of the landscape
in influencing the layout of routes and networks at different historical
stages of transport technology.

The *Journal of Transport History* and the *Journal of Economic History*
are the most comprehensive general journals.

Chapter 2

The marked revival of interest in inland waterways during recent years
had led to a large number of books about their historical origins. Of
prime importance is the series *Canals of the British Isles* published by
David and Charles, which includes Boyes (1973), Hadfield (1966 [two
titles], 1967 [two titles], 1969, 1973); and Hadfield and Biddle (1970).
Shorter accounts include L. T. C. Rolt (1950 and 1969) and C. Hadfield
(1959). On a more limited tropic there is J. R. Ward (1974). The most
comprehensive Atlas is J. Cranfield and M. Bonfiel (1966). Among older
accounts, S. Smiles (1861–2) is the most widely quoted.

Chapters 3 and 4

There is an immense bibliography on the evolution of the railways in
Britain including economic histories, historical geographies, biographies
of leading figures and simple narrative accounts. Some of the best general

accounts are listed at the end of Chapter 1. The most comprehensive
list of source material is found in G. Ottley (1965). Statistics are
summarized in B. R. Mitchell and P. Dean (1962). Good general railway
histories include C. H. Ellis (1959), J. Simmons (1968), and H. Pollins
(1971). On more specialized topics A. M. Wellington (1877) is a classic
discussion of the alignment of routes. A. W. Kirkaldy and A. D. Evans
(1927) discuss charging theory, M. C. Reed (1974) deals with investments. The influence of the state is considered in E. Cleveland-Stevens
(1915) and by H. W. Parris (1965). The urban scene is reviewed in
J. R. Kellett (1969).

For the detailed story of the spread of the railway network H. G. Lewin
(1925 and 1936) is basic. Students of particular parts of the country are
now served by a series called 'A Regional History of the Railways of
Great Britain' published by David & Charles, Newton Abbot. These
include D. St. J. Thomas (1960), H. P. White (1961 and 1963), K. J. Hoole
(1965), and D. I. Gordon (1968). For London there are E. Course (1962)
and on a wider theme T. C. Barker and M. Robbins (1963). Histories of
the original railway companies should also be consulted. The most
detailed (but pedantically chronological) is W. W. Tomlinson (1914,
republished 1967). Others include R. W. Rush (1949), F. S. Williams
(1877, republished 1957), G. Dow (1965), C. H. Grinling (1966),
C. J. Allen (1966), E. T. MacDermott (1964), C. H. Ellis (1956),
R. W. Kidner (1952 and 1953). Recent biographies include L. T. C. Rolt
(1957 and 1960) and R. S. Lambert (1934).

Issues of Bradshaws Railway Guide for 1887, 1910, and 1938, with
maps, having recently been republished by David & Charles. Journals
with particular reference to railway history include *The Railway Gazette*,
The Railway Magazine which are still current: long-established libraries
may carry *Herapaths Railway Magazine* (1835–1903) or *The Railway
Times* (1837–1914).

Chapter 5

The Ordnance Survey publish road maps at 1/50 000 and 1/250 000 also
a National Route Planning Map in two sheets at 1/625 000. On all these
maps the capacity of roads as expressed by the number of carriageways
and their function, according to the official classification, are clearly
shown. The *Annual Abstract of Statistics* (Central Statistical Office,
H.M.S.O., London) includes data on road and rail traffic, while for road
only, *Basic Road Statistics* of the British Road Federation is useful. The
Department of the Environment published a *Survey of the transport of
goods by road 1967–8* in 1972 (H.M.S.O., London).

Much of the discussion on road transport is found in journals of which,
in addition to Journals listed in Chapter 1, the *Journal of Transport
Economics and Policy* and the *Journal of the Institute of Transport
and Regional Studies* are the most valuable.

Chapter 6

H. J. Dyos and D. H. Aldcroft (1969) provide the most comprehensive recent bibliography to the article literature on port development while J. Bird (1963) propounds a most useful geographical model of the spatial development of British ports. For a more detailed study of a particular port see J. Bird (1957) and F. E. Hyde (1971). A. D. Couper (1972) discusses port development in general and C. E. Gibson (1958) deals with the changing needs of ships. For British ports see J. Bird (1963), G. Alexanderrson and G. Norstöm (1963) and H. Rees (1958). K. R. Sealy (1966) gives a most valuable coverage of air transport development. The journal *Dock and Harbour Authority* monitors current port developments and includes general articles on their economic problems.

Chapter 7

N. R. Elliott and B. Fullerton (1973) give a short general survey and bibliography of current developments in British transport. The demand for transport is analysed in B. T. Bayliss and S. L. Edwards (1970), M. Chisholm and P. O'Sullivan (1973), and S. L. Edwards and B. T. Bayliss (1971). On the restructuring of the rail network D. H. Aldcroft (1968) and G. Freeman Allen (1966) should be consulted. Motorways in general are discussed in J. Drake, H. L. Yeadon, and D. I. Evans (1970).

C. D. Foster (1963) and K. M. Gwilliam (1964) discuss general problems of transport policy. Specific aspects of these problems are covered in a series of White Papers (Ministry of Transport, Scottish Office, Welsh Office) and Royal Commission Reports (Rochdale 1962, Roskill 1971).

References

Aldcroft, D. H. (1968) *British Railways in transition, the Economic Problems of Britain's Railways since 1914,* London.

Alexandersson G. and Norström, G. (1963) *World Shipping, an Economic Geography of Ports and Seaborne Trade,* Stockholm.

Allen, C. J. (1966) *The Great Eastern Railway,* London (5th ed.).

Appleton, J. H. (1962) *The Geography of Communications in Great Britain,* London.

Barker, T. C. and Robbins, M. (1963) *A History of London Transport,* vol. i, London.

Bayliss, B. T. and Edwards, S. L. (1970) *Industrial Demand for Transport,* London.

Bird, J. H. (1957) *The Geography of the Port of London,* London.

– (1963) *The Major Seaports of the United Kingdom,* London.

– (1971) *Seaports and Seaport Terminals,* London.

Boyes, J. H. (1973) *The Canals of Eastern England,* Newton Abbot.

Bowes (1958) *Report of the Committee of Inquiry into Inland Waterways,* Cmnd. 846, London (H.M.S.O.).

Briggs, K. (1972) *Introducing Transportation Networks,* London.

British Railways Board (1963) *The Reshaping of British Railways,* London.

– (1965) *The Development of the major Railway Trunk Routes,* London.

British Waterways Board (1965) *The facts about the waterways,* London.

Brown's Export List (a monthly gazette published in Newcastle and available in Newcastle City Library).

Buchanan, C. D. (1963) *Traffic in towns,* London.

Van Den Burg, G. (1969) *Containerization—a Modern Transport System,* London.

Chisholm, M. D. I., and O'Sullivan, P. (1973) *Freight Flows and Spatial Aspects of the British Economy,* Cambridge.

Christaller, W. (1933) *Central Places in Southern Germany,* transl. C. W. Baskin, Englewood Cliffs, 1966.

Clapham, Sir J. H. (1921) *The Economic Development of France and Germany,* Cambridge.

– (1926–38) *An Economic History of Modern Britain,* 3 vols., Cambridge.

Cleveland-Stevens, E. (1915) *English Railways, their Development and their Relation to the State,* London.

Cole, J. P. and King, C. A. M. (1968) *Quantitative Geography,* London.

Collingwood, R. G. and Myres, J. N. L. (1936) *Roman Britain and the English settlements,* Oxford.

Couper, A. D. (1972) *The Geography of Sea Transport,* London.

Course, E. A. (1962) *London Railways,* London.

Cranfield, J. and Bonfiel, M. (1966) *Waterways Atlas of the British Isles,* London.

Dept. of the Environment (1972) *A Survey of the Transport of Goods by Road 1967–8,* London.

Dow, G. (1959–65), *Great Central,* 3 vols., London.

Drake, J., Yeadon, H. L., Evans, D. I. (1970) *Motorways,* London.

Dyos, H. J., and Aldcroft, D. H. (1969) *British Transport, an Economic Survey from the Seventeenth Century to the Twentieth,* Leicester.

Edwards, S. L., and Bayliss, B. T. (1971) *Operating Costs in Road Freight Transport,* H.M.S.O., London.

Ellis, C. H. (1956) *The South Western Railway, its Mechanical History and Background 1838–1922,* London.

– (1959) *British Railway History 1836–1949,* London.

Elliott, N. R., and Fullerton, B. (1973) *Transport* in House, J. W. (ed.), *The U.K. Space,* London.

Fishlow, A. (1965) *American Railroads and the Transformation of the Antebellum Economy,* Cambridge, Mass.

Fogel, R. W. (1964) *Railroads and American Economic Growth: Essays in Econometric History,* Baltimore.

Foster, C. D. (1963) *The Transport Problem,* London.

Freeman Allen, G. (1966) *British Railways after Beeching,* London.

Gibson, C. E. (1958), *The Story of the Ship,* London.

Girard, L. (1965) 'Transport' in Habakkuk H. J. and Poston M. (eds.), *The Cambridge Economic History of Europe,* Cambridge.

Gordon, D. I. (1968) *The Eastern Counties,* Newton Abbot.

Grinling, C. H. (1966) *History of the Great Northern Railway 1845– 1922,* London.

Gwilliam, K. M. (1964) *Transport and Public Policy,* London.

Hadfield, E. C. R. (1959) *British canals, an illustrated history,* Newton Abbot (2nd. ed.).

– (1966) *The Canals of the East Midlands including Parts of London,* Newton Abbot.

– (1966) *The Canals of the West Midlands,* Newton Abbot.

– (1967) *The Canals of South Wales and the Border,* Newton Abbot.

– (1967) *The Canals of South West England,* Newton Abbot.

– (1969) *The Canals of South and South East England,* Newton Abbot.

– (1973) *The Canals of Yorkshire and North East England,* Newton Abbot.

– and Biddle, G. (1970) *The Canals of North West England,* Newton Abbot.

Haggett, P. (1965) *Locational Analysis in Human Geography,* London.

– and Chorley, R. J. (1969) *Network Analysis in Geography,* London.

Hawke, G. R. (1970) *Railways and Economic Growth in England and Wales 1840–70,* Oxford.

Hay, A. (1973) *Transport for the space economy, a Geographical Study,* London.

Hibbs, J. (1968) *The History of British Bus Services,* Newton Abbot.

Hoole, K. J. (1965) *The North East,* Newton Abbot.

Horton, F. (ed.) (1968) *Geographic studies of urban transportation and network analysis* Northwestern Univ. Studies in Geography No. 16 Chicago.

Hyde, F. E. (1971) *Liverpool and the Mersey, an Economic History of a Port, 1700–1970,* Newton Abbot.

Jackman, W. T. (1916) *The Development of Transportation in Modern England,* Cambridge (reprinted 1962).

Kansky, K. J. (1963) *Structure of Transporation Networks: Relationships between Network Geometry and Regional Characteristics,* Chicago.

Kellett, J. R. (1969) *The Impact of Railways on Victorian Cities ,* London.

Kidner, R. W. (1952) *The London, Chatham and Dover Railway,* South Godstone.

– (1953) *The South Eastern Railway and the South East and Central Railway,* South Godstone.

Kirkaldy, A. W. and Evans, A. D. (1927) *The History and Economics of Transport,* London (4th ed.).

Lambert, R. S. (1934) *The Railway King 1800–1871. G. Hudson,* London.

Lewin, H. G. (1925) *Early British Railways 1801–44,* London.

– (1936) *The Railway Mania and its Aftermath 1845–52,* rev. edn. Newton Abbot, 1968.

Macdermot, E. T. (1964) *History of the Great Western Railway,* rev. edn., ed. C. R. Clinker, Shepperton.

Marshall, J. (1969–72) *The Lancashire and Yorkshire Railway* 3 vols., Newton Abbot.

Ministry of Transport (1963) *Rural transport surveys,* London.

– (1966) *Transport policy,* Cmnd 3057, London.

– (1967) *Public transport and traffic,* Cmnd 3481, London.

– (1967) *Railway policy,* Cmnd 3439, London.

– (1967) *The transport of freight,* Cmnd 3470, London.

– (1970) *Roads for the Future, The New Inter-Urban Plan for England,* Cmnd 4369, London.

Mitchell, B. R., and Deane, P. (1962) *Abstract of British Historical Statistics,* Cambridge.

Mitchell, B. R., and Jones, H. G. (1971) *Second Abstract of British Historical Statistics,* Cambridge.

National Ports Council (1972) *Port Statistics,* London.

Nock, O. S. (1961) *The South Eastern and Chatham railway,* London.

Ottley, G. (1965) *A Bibliography of British Railway History,* London.

Parris, H. W. (1965) *Government and the railways in Nineteenth-Century Britain,* London.

Pollins, H. (1971) *Britian's Railways, an Industrial History,* Newton Abbot.

Pratt, E. A. (1912) *A History of Inland Transport and Communication,* reprinted Newton Abbot 1970.

Reed, M. C. (1974) *Investments in Railways in Britain*, London.

Rees, H. (1958) *British Ports and Shipping*, London.

Reilly, W. J. (1929) *Methods for the study of retail relationships*, Austin, Texas.

Rochdale (1962) *Report of the Committee of Inquiry into the Major Seaports of Great Britain* Cmnd 1824, H.M.S.O., London.

Rolt, L. T. C. (1950) *The Inland Waterways of England*, London.

— (1957) *Isambard Kingdom Brunel, a Biography*, London.

— (1960) *George and Robert Stephenson: the Railway Revolution*, London.

— (1969) *Navigable waterways*, London.

Roskill (1971) *Report of the Commission on the Third London Airport*, H.M.S.O., London.

Rush, R. W. (1949) *The Lancashire and Yorkshire Railway and its Locomotives, 1846–1923*, London.

Sargent, J. R. (1958) *British Transport Policy*, Oxford.

Savage, C. I. (1966) *An Economic History of Transport*, London (rev. edn.).

Scottish Office (1969) *Scottish roads in the 1970s*, Cmnd 3953, H.M.S.O., Edinburgh.

Sealy K. R. (1966) *The Geography of Air Transport*, London.

Sherrington, C. E. R. (1928) *Economics of Rail Transport in Great Britain*, London.

Simmons, J. (1962), *Transport*, London.

— (1968) *The Railways of Britain, an Historical Introduction*, London.

Smiles, S. (1861–2) *Lives of the Engineers with an Account of their Principal Works*, London (3 vols.).

Smith, W. (1949) *An Historical Introduction to the Economic Geography of Great Britain*, reprinted London 1968.

Taaffe, E. J., and Gauthier, H. L. (1973) *Geography of Transportation* Englewood Cliffs.

Thomas, D. St. J. (1960) *The West Country*, London.

Tomlinson, W. W. (1914) *The North Eastern Railway, Its Rise and Development* new ed., Newton Abbot, 1967.

Walters, A. A. (1968) *Integration in Freight Transport*, London.

Ward, J. K. (1974) *The Finance of Canal Building in Eighteenth-century England*, Oxford.

Weber, A. (1909) translated as *Theory of the Location of Industries*, Chicago, 1926.

Wellington, A. M. (1877) *The Economic Theory of Railway Location*, New York.

Welsh Office (1967) *Wales, the Way Ahead*, Cmnd 3334, H.M.S.O., Cardiff.

White H. P. (1961) *Southern England*, Newton Abbot.

— (1963) *Greater London*, Newton Abbot.

Williams, F. S. (1877) *The Midland Railway, its Rise and Progress: a Narrative of Modern Enterprise*, republished Newton Abbot, 1967.

Williams, R. A. (1968–73) *The London and South Western Railway*, Newton Abbot.

Index